GHOST WORLD

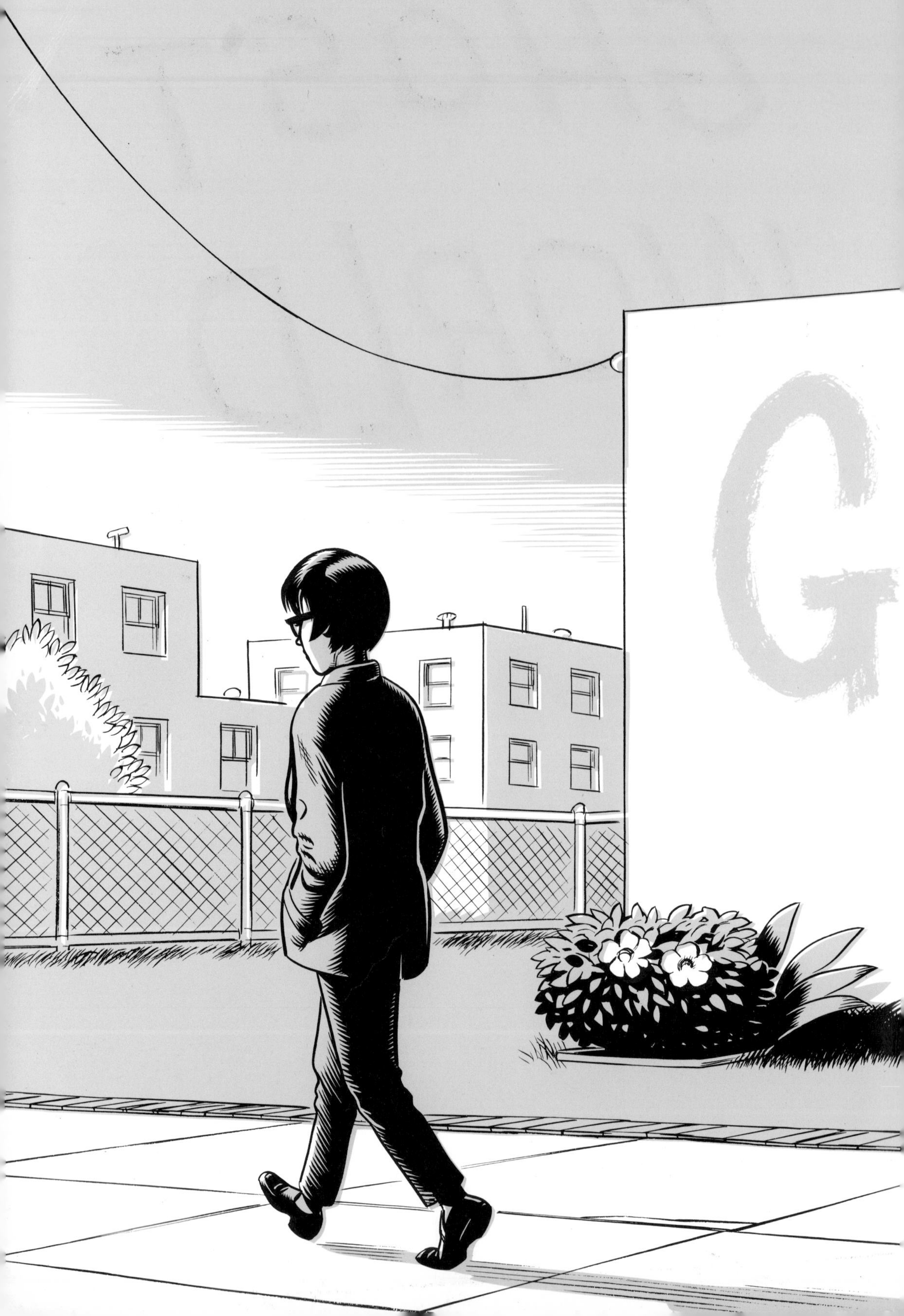
G

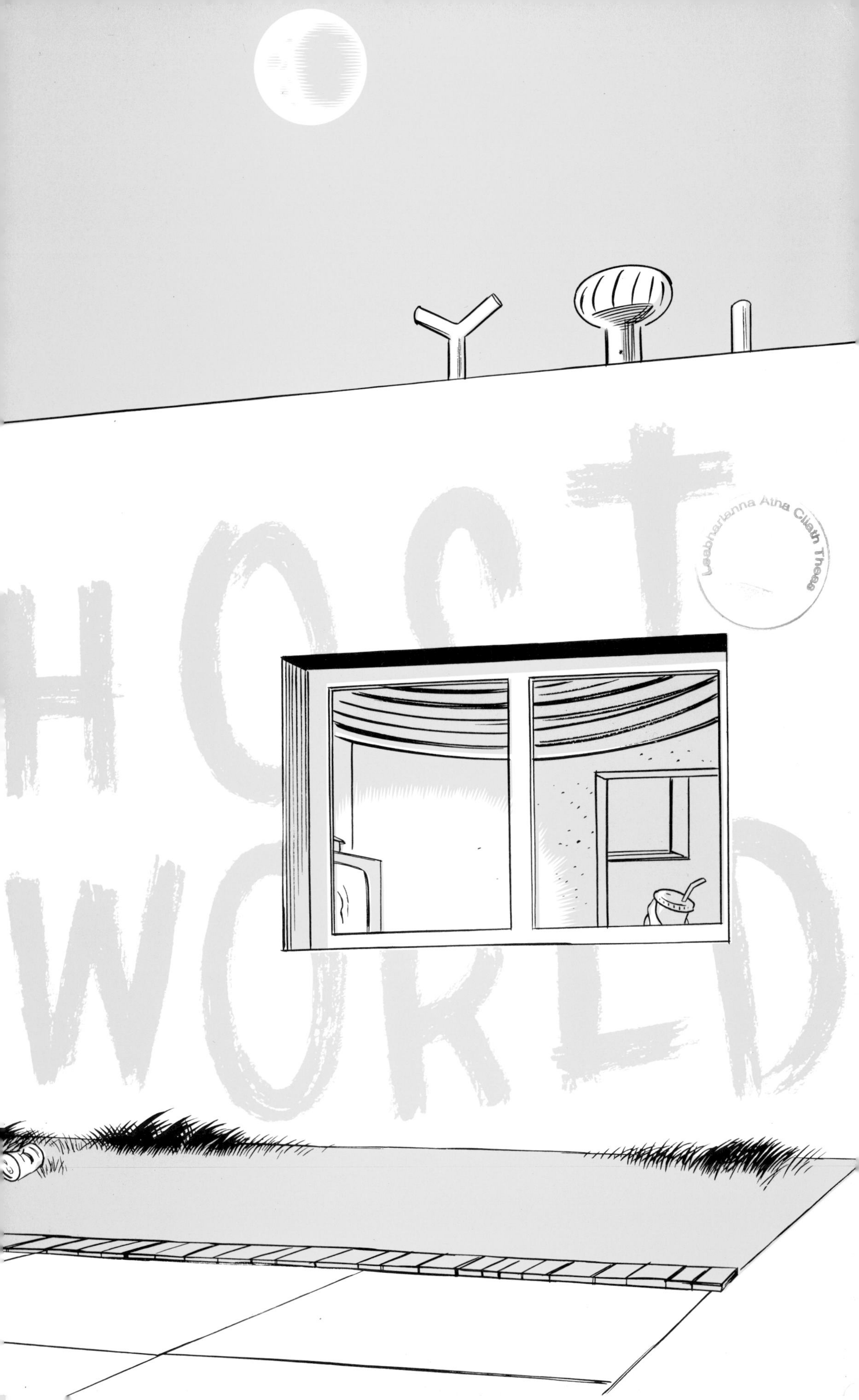
HOST
WORLD

BOOKS BY DANIEL CLOWES

NOVELS

Like A Velvet Glove Cast in Iron

Pussey!

SHORT STORIES

Lout Rampage!

Orgy Bound

ANTHOLOGIES

The Manly World of Lloyd Llewellyn

#$@&!

ABSOLUTELY NORMAL
ANY MOONS
ENCYCLOPEDIA of UNUSUAL SEX PRACT
CRAZYWILD
SAGE
NOTHING-AT-ALL
GDG
THE VERY THING THAT HAPPENS
2000 INSULTS
OEDIPUS REX
USED
THE WORLD OF HENRY ORIENT
France Gall · volume 2
AGNES MOUTHWASH

for
Erika

Designed by D. CLOWES
First Published by THOMPSON & GROTH
COLOR SEPARATIONS BY JOHN KURAMOTO
SPECIAL THANKS TO CHAS· SCHNEIDER
All contents © 1993, 1994, 1995,
1996, 1997 Daniel Clowes

Daniel Clowes has asserted his right under the Copyright, Designs and
Patents Act 1988 to be identified as the author of this work

Permission to reproduce material for any reason must be
obtained from the author or his publisher

First published in Great Britain in 2000 by

JONATHAN CAPE

Random House, 20 Vauxhall Bridge Road, London SW1V 2SA
www.randomhouse.co.uk

The Random House Group Limited Reg. No. 954009

A CIP catalogue record for this book
is available from the British Library

ISBN 0-224-06088-0

Printed and bound in Slovenia
by MKT PRINT d.d.

CONTENTS

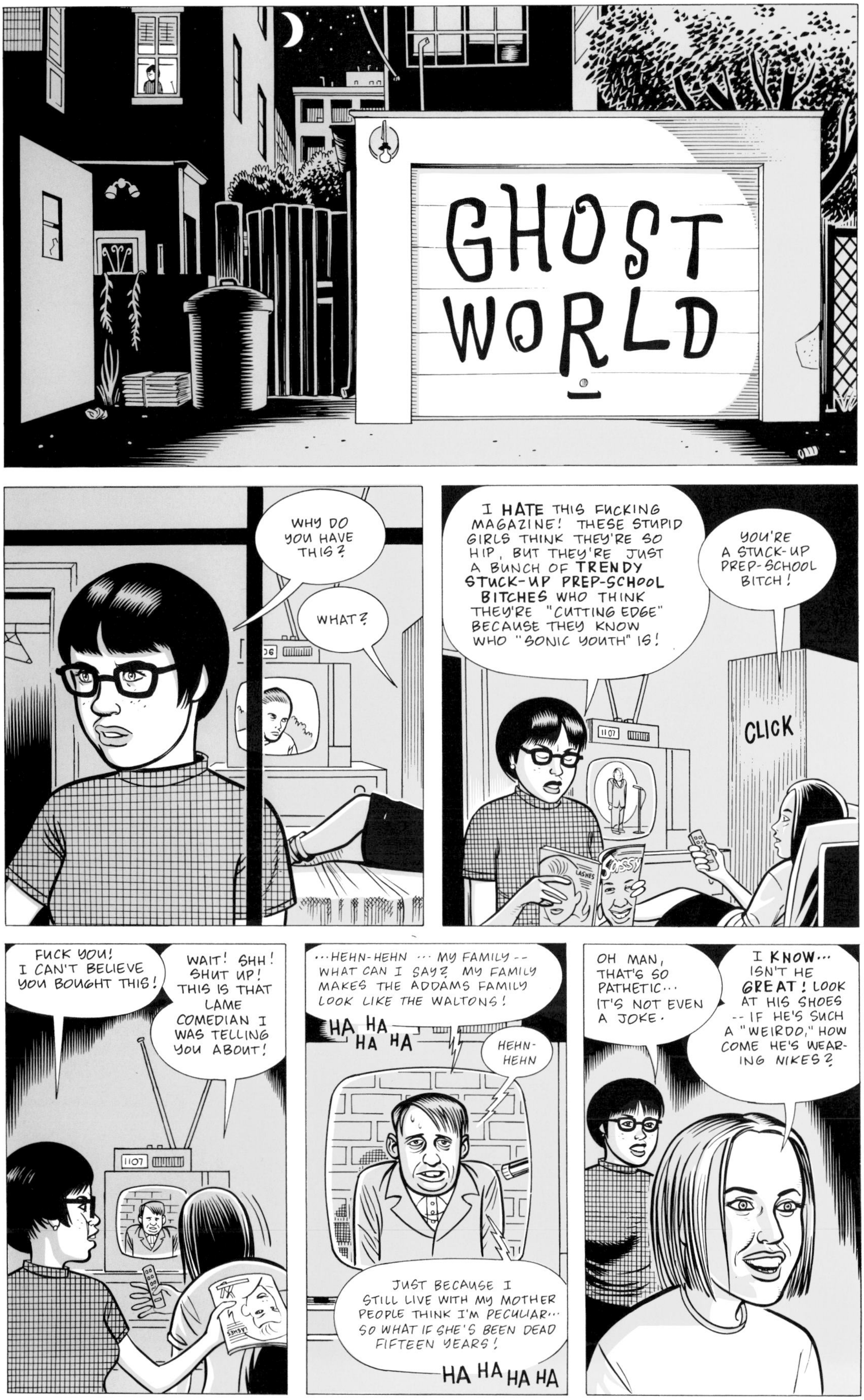
GHOST WORLD
WHY DO YOU HAVE THIS?
WHAT?
I HATE THIS FUCKING MAGAZINE! THESE STUPID GIRLS THINK THEY'RE SO HIP, BUT THEY'RE JUST A BUNCH OF TRENDY STUCK-UP PREP-SCHOOL BITCHES WHO THINK THEY'RE "CUTTING EDGE" BECAUSE THEY KNOW WHO "SONIC YOUTH" IS!
YOU'RE A STUCK-UP PREP-SCHOOL BITCH!
CLICK
FUCK YOU! I CAN'T BELIEVE YOU BOUGHT THIS!
WAIT! SHH! SHUT UP! THIS IS THAT LAME COMEDIAN I WAS TELLING YOU ABOUT!
...HEHN-HEHN ... MY FAMILY -- WHAT CAN I SAY? MY FAMILY MAKES THE ADDAMS FAMILY LOOK LIKE THE WALTONS!
HA HA HA HA
HEHN-HEHN
JUST BECAUSE I STILL LIVE WITH MY MOTHER PEOPLE THINK I'M PECULIAR... SO WHAT IF SHE'S BEEN DEAD FIFTEEN YEARS!
HA HA HA HA
OH MAN, THAT'S SO PATHETIC... IT'S NOT EVEN A JOKE.
I KNOW... ISN'T HE GREAT! LOOK AT HIS SHOES -- IF HE'S SUCH A "WEIRDO," HOW COME HE'S WEARING NIKES?

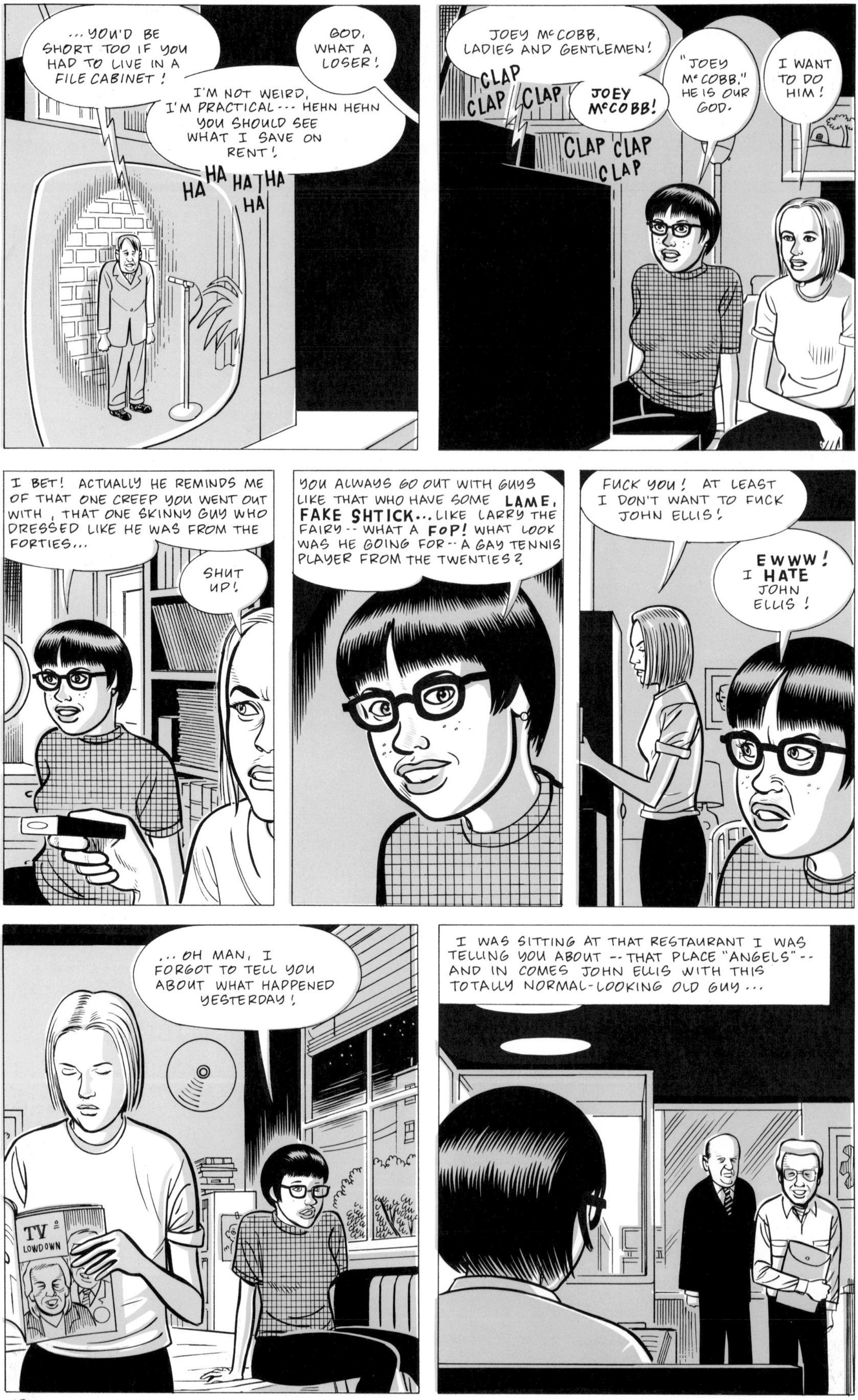

...YOU'D BE SHORT TOO IF YOU HAD TO LIVE IN A FILE CABINET!
I'M NOT WEIRD, I'M PRACTICAL--- HEHN HEHN YOU SHOULD SEE WHAT I SAVE ON RENT!
GOD, WHAT A LOSER!
HA HA HA HA HA
JOEY McCOBB, LADIES AND GENTLEMEN!
CLAP CLAP CLAP
JOEY McCOBB!
CLAP CLAP CLAP
"JOEY McCOBB," HE IS OUR GOD.
I WANT TO DO HIM!
I BET! ACTUALLY HE REMINDS ME OF THAT ONE CREEP YOU WENT OUT WITH, THAT ONE SKINNY GUY WHO DRESSED LIKE HE WAS FROM THE FORTIES...
SHUT UP!
YOU ALWAYS GO OUT WITH GUYS LIKE THAT WHO HAVE SOME LAME, FAKE SHTICK...LIKE LARRY THE FAIRY -- WHAT A FOP! WHAT LOOK WAS HE GOING FOR -- A GAY TENNIS PLAYER FROM THE TWENTIES?
FUCK YOU! AT LEAST I DON'T WANT TO FUCK JOHN ELLIS!
EWWW! I HATE JOHN ELLIS!
...OH MAN, I FORGOT TO TELL YOU ABOUT WHAT HAPPENED YESTERDAY!
TV LOWDOWN
I WAS SITTING AT THAT RESTAURANT I WAS TELLING YOU ABOUT -- THAT PLACE "ANGELS" -- AND IN COMES JOHN ELLIS WITH THIS TOTALLY NORMAL-LOOKING OLD GUY...

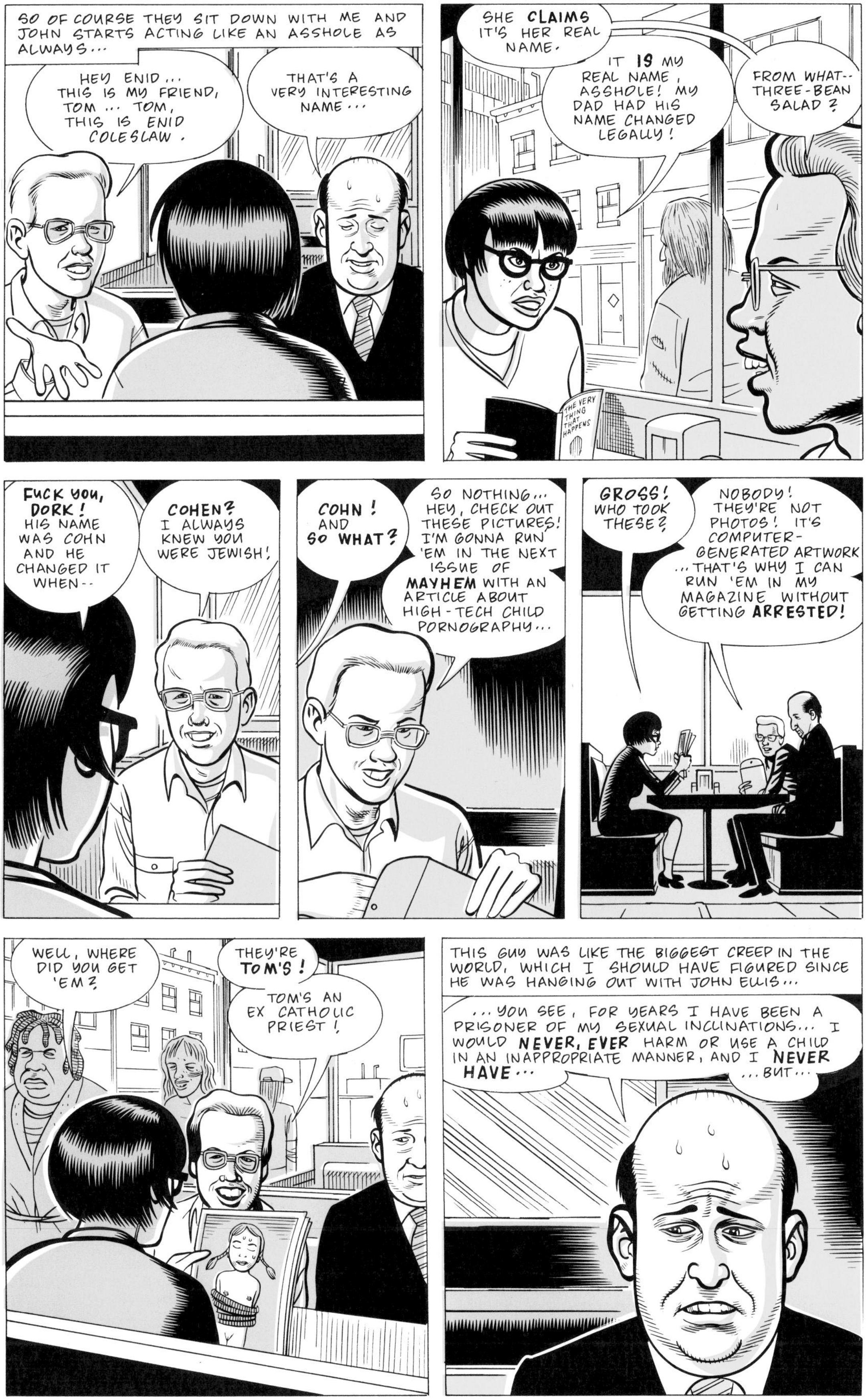

SO OF COURSE THEY SIT DOWN WITH ME AND JOHN STARTS ACTING LIKE AN ASSHOLE AS ALWAYS...
HEY ENID... THIS IS MY FRIEND, TOM... TOM, THIS IS ENID COLESLAW.
THAT'S A VERY INTERESTING NAME...
SHE CLAIMS IT'S HER REAL NAME.
IT IS MY REAL NAME, ASSHOLE! MY DAD HAD HIS NAME CHANGED LEGALLY!
FROM WHAT-- THREE-BEAN SALAD?
THE VERY THING THAT HAPPENS
FUCK YOU, DORK! HIS NAME WAS COHN AND HE CHANGED IT WHEN--
COHEN? I ALWAYS KNEW YOU WERE JEWISH!
COHN! AND SO WHAT?
SO NOTHING... HEY, CHECK OUT THESE PICTURES! I'M GONNA RUN 'EM IN THE NEXT ISSUE OF MAYHEM WITH AN ARTICLE ABOUT HIGH-TECH CHILD PORNOGRAPHY...
GROSS! WHO TOOK THESE?
NOBODY! THEY'RE NOT PHOTOS! IT'S COMPUTER-GENERATED ARTWORK ...THAT'S WHY I CAN RUN 'EM IN MY MAGAZINE WITHOUT GETTING ARRESTED!
WELL, WHERE DID YOU GET 'EM?
THEY'RE TOM'S!
TOM'S AN EX CATHOLIC PRIEST!
THIS GUY WAS LIKE THE BIGGEST CREEP IN THE WORLD, WHICH I SHOULD HAVE FIGURED SINCE HE WAS HANGING OUT WITH JOHN ELLIS...
...YOU SEE, FOR YEARS I HAVE BEEN A PRISONER OF MY SEXUAL INCLINATIONS... I WOULD NEVER, EVER HARM OR USE A CHILD IN AN INAPPROPRIATE MANNER, AND I NEVER HAVE...
...BUT...

...BUT... NONE OF US HAS ANY CONTROL OVER OUR PARTICULAR DESIRES, AND NOW, THANKS TO THE VERISIMILITUDE OF THESE COMPUTER-GENERATED IMAGES I AM ABLE TO ATTAIN MATERIAL THAT INDULGES MY SPECIFIC FANTASIES WITHOUT CAUSING HARM OR DAMAGE TO ANYONE...

HEY TOM, ENID'S ONLY EIGHTEEN!

FUCK YOU, JOHN!

GOD, WHAT AN ASSHOLE...

WHY DIDN'T YOU TELL ME ABOUT THAT RIGHT AWAY?

I WAS GOING TO, BUT I KNOW YOU THINK I HAVE A CRUSH ON JOHN ELLIS...

I DON'T REALLY THINK THAT... YOU DON'T, DO YOU?

DON'T WORRY!

...SO WHAT'S THE DEAL WITH HIM, IS HE LIKE A NAZI?

YEAH, I DUNNO... HE SAYS HE "HATES EVERY-BODY EQUALLY" BUT I KNOW HE WRITES FAN LETTERS TO MASS MURDERERS AND HANGS OUT WITH KKK GUYS AND STUFF...

GOD, HE NEEDS TO GET LAID!

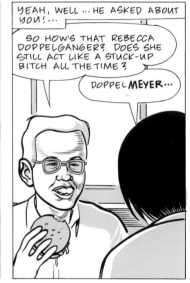

YEAH, WELL... HE ASKED ABOUT YOU!...

SO HOW'S THAT REBECCA DOPPELGANGER? DOES SHE STILL ACT LIKE A STUCK-UP BITCH ALL THE TIME?

DOPPELMEYER...

EVEN I'M NOT THAT DESPERATE!

OH YEAH, LIKE YOU COULDN'T HAVE ANY GUY IN THE WORLD IF YOU WEREN'T SO FUCKIN' PICKY... YOU'RE A SKINNY, BLOND WASP--THAT'S WHAT EVERY GUY WANTS!

I'M NOT A WASP!

HEY, DID I TELL YOU ABOUT THAT SATANIST COUPLE THAT COMES INTO ANGEL'S?

I THINK SO...

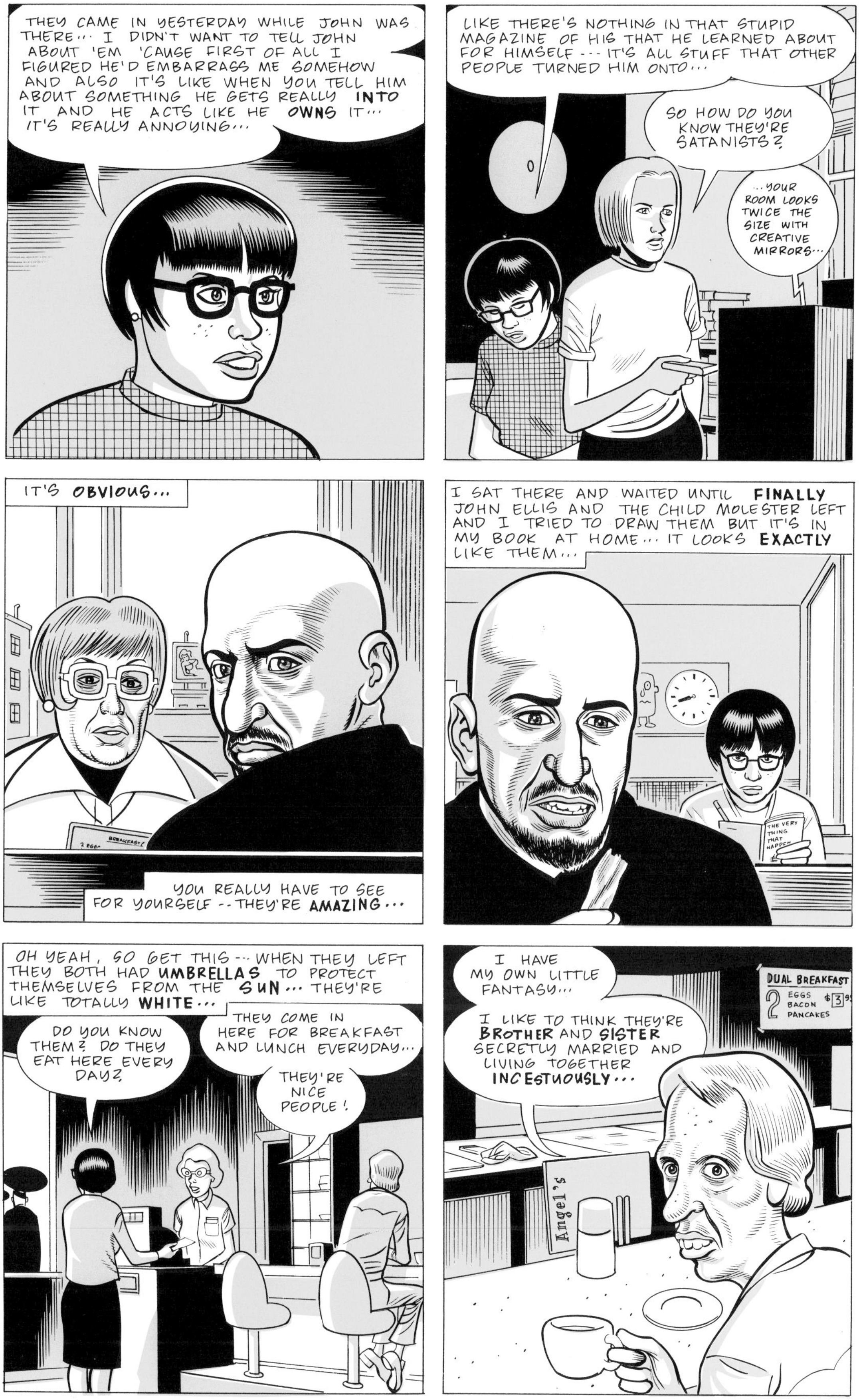
THEY CAME IN YESTERDAY WHILE JOHN WAS THERE... I DIDN'T WANT TO TELL JOHN ABOUT 'EM 'CAUSE FIRST OF ALL I FIGURED HE'D EMBARRASS ME SOMEHOW AND ALSO IT'S LIKE WHEN YOU TELL HIM ABOUT SOMETHING HE GETS REALLY **INTO** IT AND HE ACTS LIKE HE **OWNS** IT... IT'S REALLY ANNOYING...
LIKE THERE'S NOTHING IN THAT STUPID MAGAZINE OF HIS THAT HE LEARNED ABOUT FOR HIMSELF --- IT'S ALL STUFF THAT OTHER PEOPLE TURNED HIM ONTO...
SO HOW DO YOU KNOW THEY'RE SATANISTS?
...YOUR ROOM LOOKS TWICE THE SIZE WITH CREATIVE MIRRORS...
IT'S **OBVIOUS**...
YOU REALLY HAVE TO SEE FOR YOURSELF -- THEY'RE **AMAZING**...
I SAT THERE AND WAITED UNTIL **FINALLY** JOHN ELLIS AND THE CHILD MOLESTER LEFT AND I TRIED TO DRAW THEM BUT IT'S IN MY BOOK AT HOME... IT LOOKS **EXACTLY** LIKE THEM...
OH YEAH, SO GET THIS -- WHEN THEY LEFT THEY BOTH HAD **UMBRELLAS** TO PROTECT THEMSELVES FROM THE **SUN**... THEY'RE LIKE TOTALLY **WHITE**...
DO YOU KNOW THEM? DO THEY EAT HERE EVERY DAY?
THEY COME IN HERE FOR BREAKFAST AND LUNCH EVERYDAY...
THEY'RE NICE PEOPLE!
I HAVE MY OWN LITTLE FANTASY...
I LIKE TO THINK THEY'RE **BROTHER** AND **SISTER** SECRETLY MARRIED AND LIVING TOGETHER **INCESTUOUSLY**...
DUAL BREAKFAST
2 EGGS BACON PANCAKES $3
Angel's

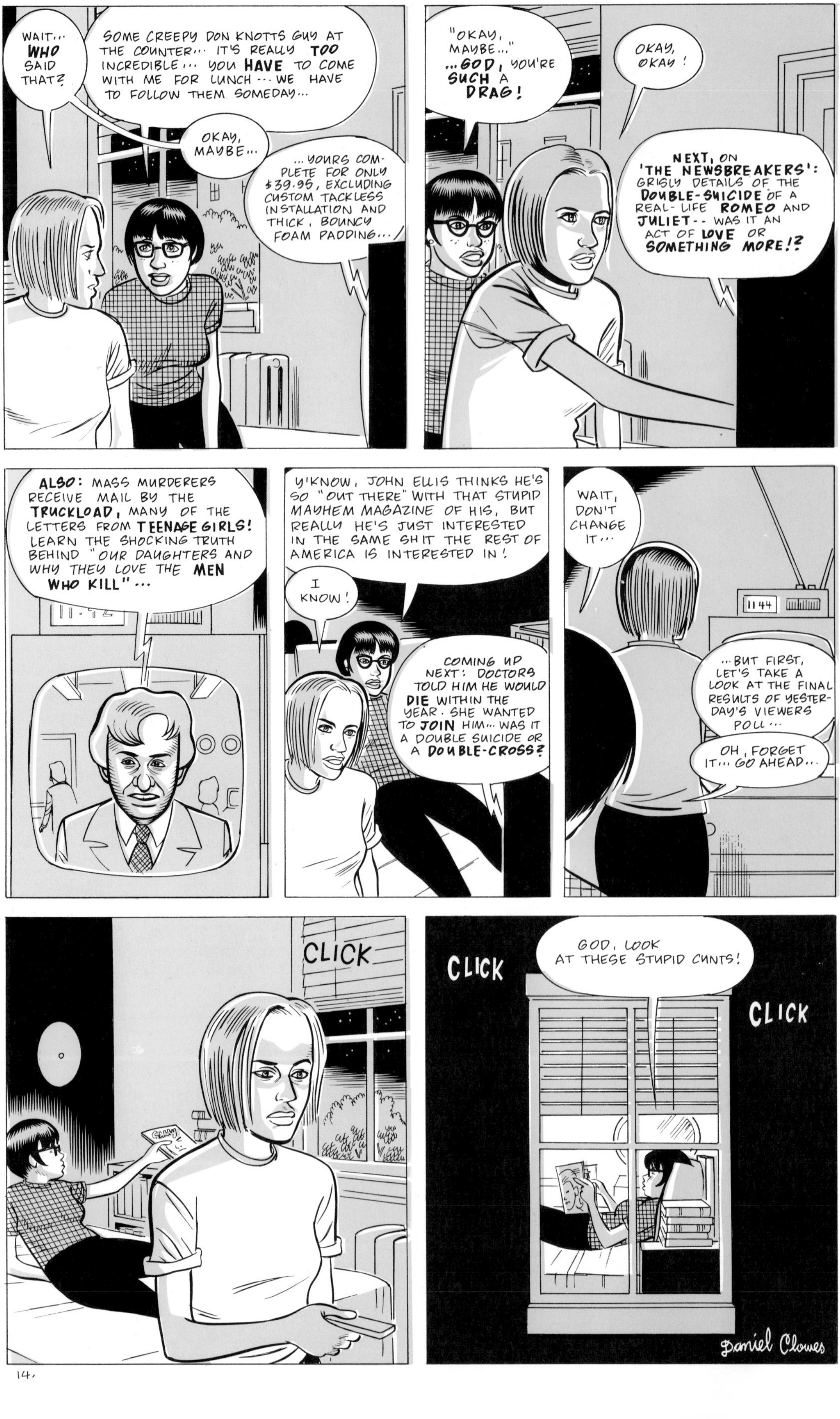
WAIT... WHO SAID THAT?
SOME CREEPY DON KNOTTS GUY AT THE COUNTER... IT'S REALLY TOO INCREDIBLE... YOU HAVE TO COME WITH ME FOR LUNCH --- WE HAVE TO FOLLOW THEM SOMEDAY...
OKAY, MAYBE...
...YOURS COMPLETE FOR ONLY $39.95, EXCLUDING CUSTOM TACKLESS INSTALLATION AND THICK, BOUNCY FOAM PADDING...
"OKAY, MAYBE..." ...GOD, YOU'RE SUCH A DRAG!
OKAY, OKAY!
NEXT, ON 'THE NEWSBREAKERS': GRISLY DETAILS OF THE DOUBLE-SUICIDE OF A REAL-LIFE ROMEO AND JULIET-- WAS IT AN ACT OF LOVE OR SOMETHING MORE!?
ALSO: MASS MURDERERS RECEIVE MAIL BY THE TRUCKLOAD, MANY OF THE LETTERS FROM TEENAGE GIRLS! LEARN THE SHOCKING TRUTH BEHIND "OUR DAUGHTERS AND WHY THEY LOVE THE MEN WHO KILL"...
Y'KNOW, JOHN ELLIS THINKS HE'S SO "OUT THERE" WITH THAT STUPID MAYHEM MAGAZINE OF HIS, BUT REALLY HE'S JUST INTERESTED IN THE SAME SHIT THE REST OF AMERICA IS INTERESTED IN!
I KNOW!
COMING UP NEXT: DOCTORS TOLD HIM HE WOULD DIE WITHIN THE YEAR. SHE WANTED TO JOIN HIM... WAS IT A DOUBLE SUICIDE OR A DOUBLE-CROSS?
WAIT, DON'T CHANGE IT...
11:44
...BUT FIRST, LET'S TAKE A LOOK AT THE FINAL RESULTS OF YESTERDAY'S VIEWERS POLL...
OH, FORGET IT... GO AHEAD...
CLICK
CLICK
GOD, LOOK AT THESE STUPID CUNTS!
CLICK
Daniel Clowes

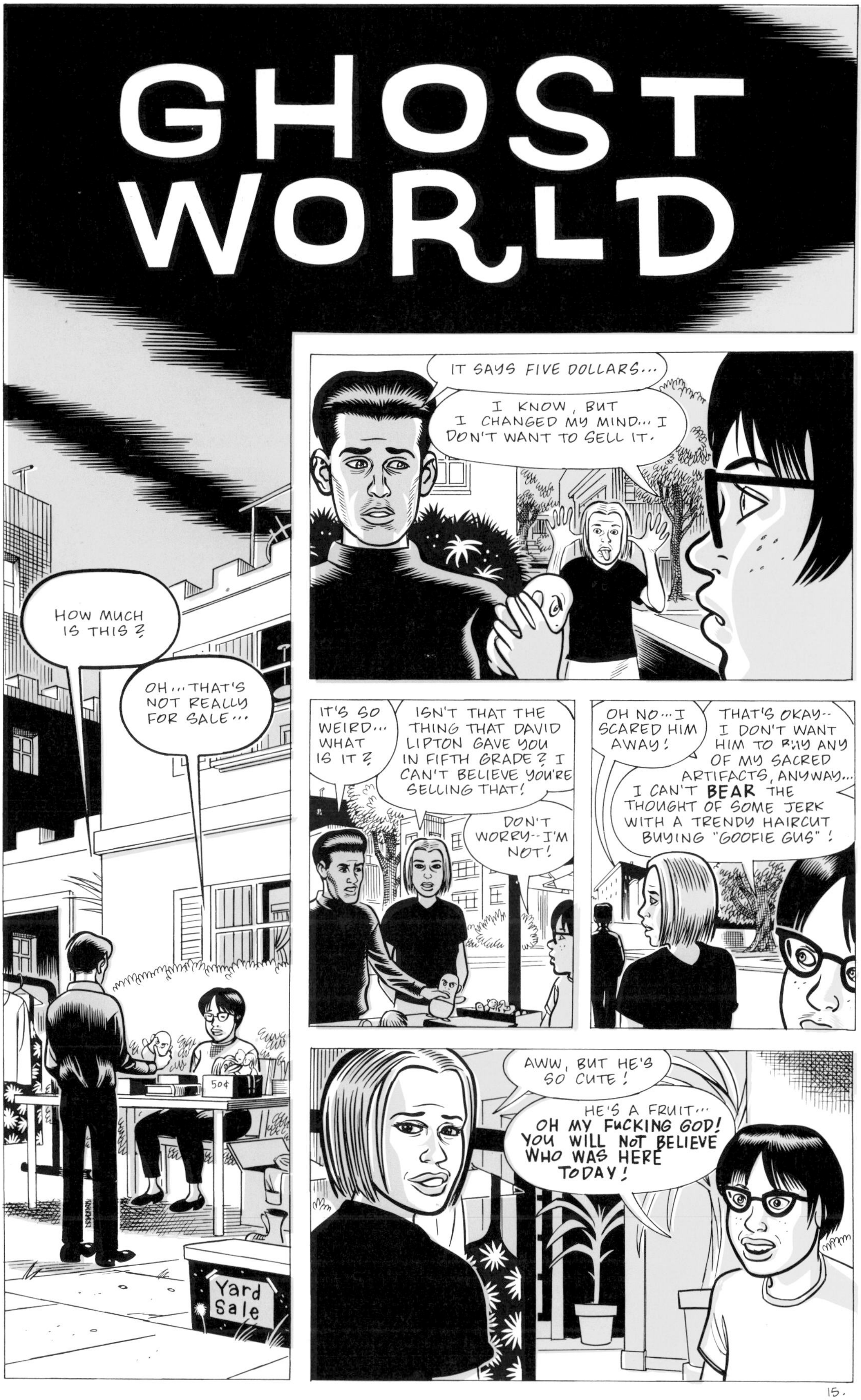
GHOST WORLD
HOW MUCH IS THIS?
OH... THAT'S NOT REALLY FOR SALE...
Yard Sale
50¢
IT SAYS FIVE DOLLARS...
I KNOW, BUT I CHANGED MY MIND... I DON'T WANT TO SELL IT.
IT'S SO WEIRD... WHAT IS IT?
ISN'T THAT THE THING THAT DAVID LIPTON GAVE YOU IN FIFTH GRADE? I CAN'T BELIEVE YOU'RE SELLING THAT!
DON'T WORRY-- I'M NOT!
OH NO... I SCARED HIM AWAY!
THAT'S OKAY-- I DON'T WANT HIM TO BUY ANY OF MY SACRED ARTIFACTS, ANYWAY... I CAN'T BEAR THE THOUGHT OF SOME JERK WITH A TRENDY HAIRCUT BUYING "GOOFIE GUS"!
AWW, BUT HE'S SO CUTE!
HE'S A FRUIT... OH MY FUCKING GOD! YOU WILL NOT BELIEVE WHO WAS HERE TODAY!

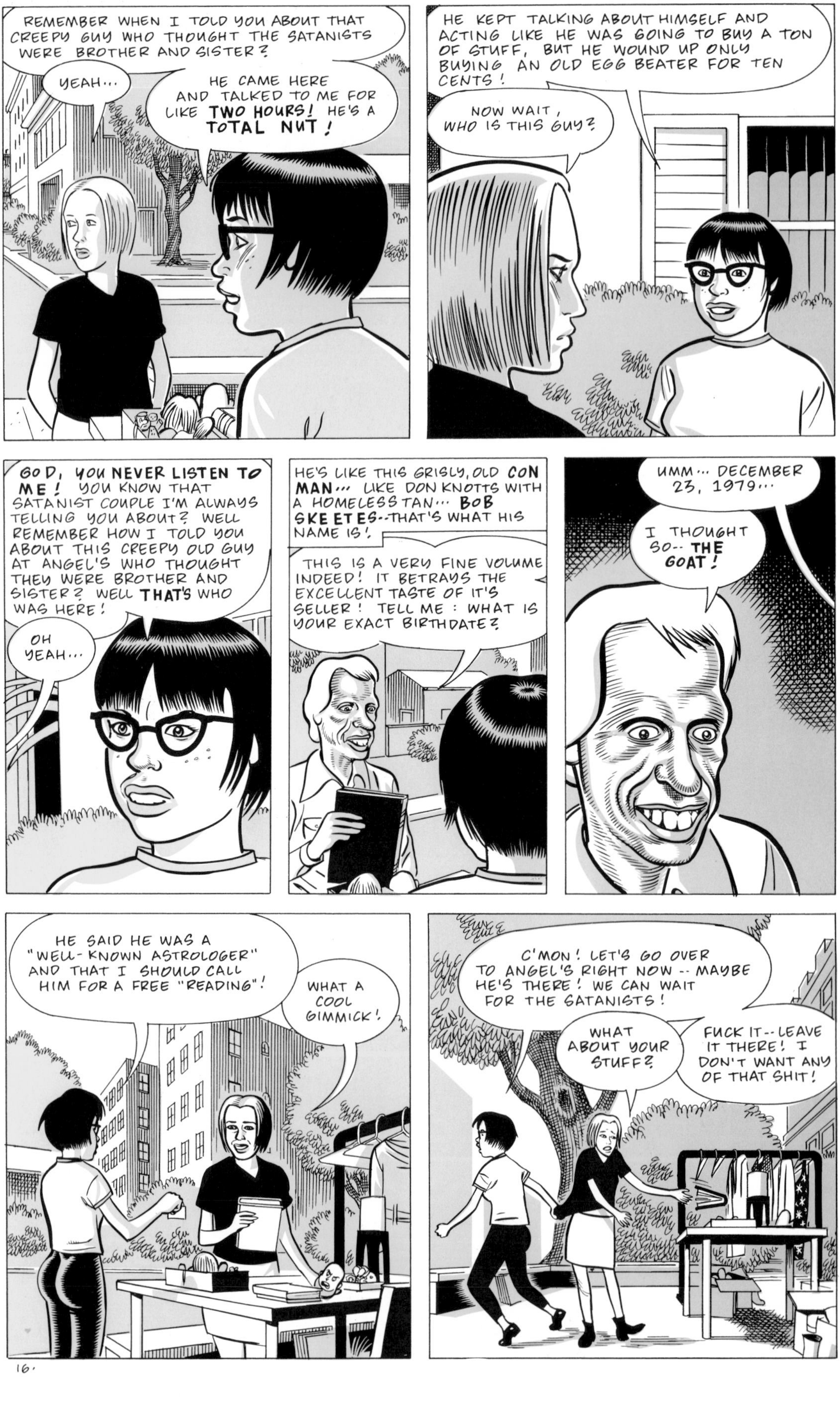
REMEMBER WHEN I TOLD YOU ABOUT THAT CREEPY GUY WHO THOUGHT THE SATANISTS WERE BROTHER AND SISTER?
YEAH...
HE CAME HERE AND TALKED TO ME FOR LIKE TWO HOURS! HE'S A TOTAL NUT!
HE KEPT TALKING ABOUT HIMSELF AND ACTING LIKE HE WAS GOING TO BUY A TON OF STUFF, BUT HE WOUND UP ONLY BUYING AN OLD EGG BEATER FOR TEN CENTS!
NOW WAIT, WHO IS THIS GUY?
GOD, YOU NEVER LISTEN TO ME! YOU KNOW THAT SATANIST COUPLE I'M ALWAYS TELLING YOU ABOUT? WELL REMEMBER HOW I TOLD YOU ABOUT THIS CREEPY OLD GUY AT ANGEL'S WHO THOUGHT THEY WERE BROTHER AND SISTER? WELL THAT'S WHO WAS HERE!
OH YEAH...
HE'S LIKE THIS GRISLY, OLD CON MAN... LIKE DON KNOTTS WITH A HOMELESS TAN... BOB SKEETES--THAT'S WHAT HIS NAME IS!
THIS IS A VERY FINE VOLUME INDEED! IT BETRAYS THE EXCELLENT TASTE OF IT'S SELLER! TELL ME: WHAT IS YOUR EXACT BIRTHDATE?
UMM... DECEMBER 23, 1979...
I THOUGHT SO-- THE GOAT!
HE SAID HE WAS A "WELL-KNOWN ASTROLOGER" AND THAT I SHOULD CALL HIM FOR A FREE "READING"!
WHAT A COOL GIMMICK!
C'MON! LET'S GO OVER TO ANGEL'S RIGHT NOW -- MAYBE HE'S THERE! WE CAN WAIT FOR THE SATANISTS!
WHAT ABOUT YOUR STUFF?
FUCK IT -- LEAVE IT THERE! I DON'T WANT ANY OF THAT SHIT!

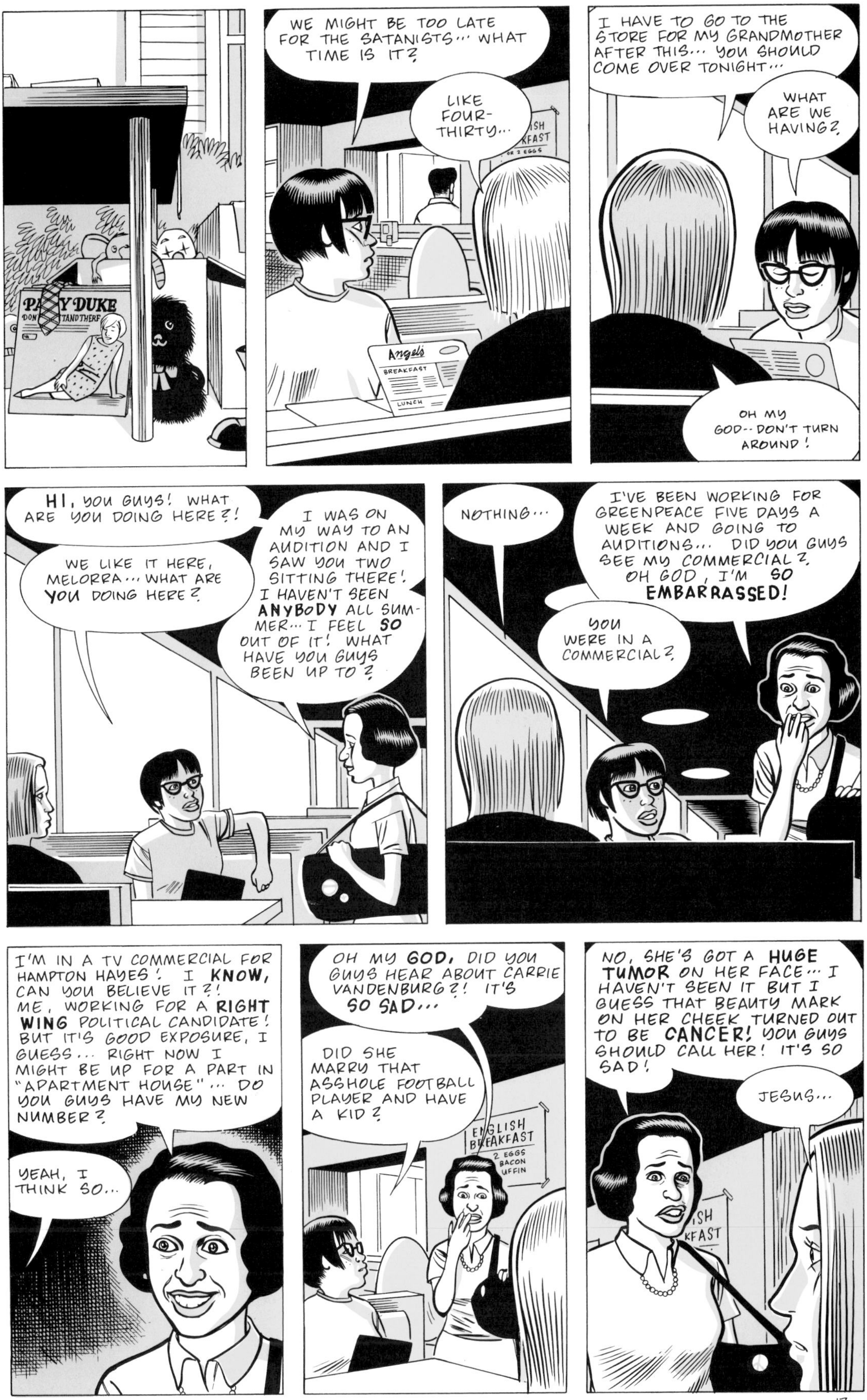
WE MIGHT BE TOO LATE FOR THE SATANISTS... WHAT TIME IS IT?
LIKE FOUR-THIRTY...
Angel's
BREAKFAST
LUNCH
I HAVE TO GO TO THE STORE FOR MY GRANDMOTHER AFTER THIS... YOU SHOULD COME OVER TONIGHT...
WHAT ARE WE HAVING?
OH MY GOD-- DON'T TURN AROUND!
HI, YOU GUYS! WHAT ARE YOU DOING HERE?!
WE LIKE IT HERE, MELORRA... WHAT ARE YOU DOING HERE?
I WAS ON MY WAY TO AN AUDITION AND I SAW YOU TWO SITTING THERE! I HAVEN'T SEEN ANYBODY ALL SUMMER... I FEEL SO OUT OF IT! WHAT HAVE YOU GUYS BEEN UP TO?
NOTHING...
I'VE BEEN WORKING FOR GREENPEACE FIVE DAYS A WEEK AND GOING TO AUDITIONS... DID YOU GUYS SEE MY COMMERCIAL? OH GOD, I'M SO EMBARRASSED!
YOU WERE IN A COMMERCIAL?
I'M IN A TV COMMERCIAL FOR HAMPTON HAYES! I KNOW, CAN YOU BELIEVE IT?! ME, WORKING FOR A RIGHT WING POLITICAL CANDIDATE! BUT IT'S GOOD EXPOSURE, I GUESS... RIGHT NOW I MIGHT BE UP FOR A PART IN "APARTMENT HOUSE"... DO YOU GUYS HAVE MY NEW NUMBER?
YEAH, I THINK SO...
OH MY GOD, DID YOU GUYS HEAR ABOUT CARRIE VANDENBURG?! IT'S SO SAD...
DID SHE MARRY THAT ASSHOLE FOOTBALL PLAYER AND HAVE A KID?
ENGLISH BREAKFAST
2 EGGS
BACON
UFFIN
NO, SHE'S GOT A HUGE TUMOR ON HER FACE... I HAVEN'T SEEN IT BUT I GUESS THAT BEAUTY MARK ON HER CHEEK TURNED OUT TO BE CANCER! YOU GUYS SHOULD CALL HER! IT'S SO SAD!
JESUS...

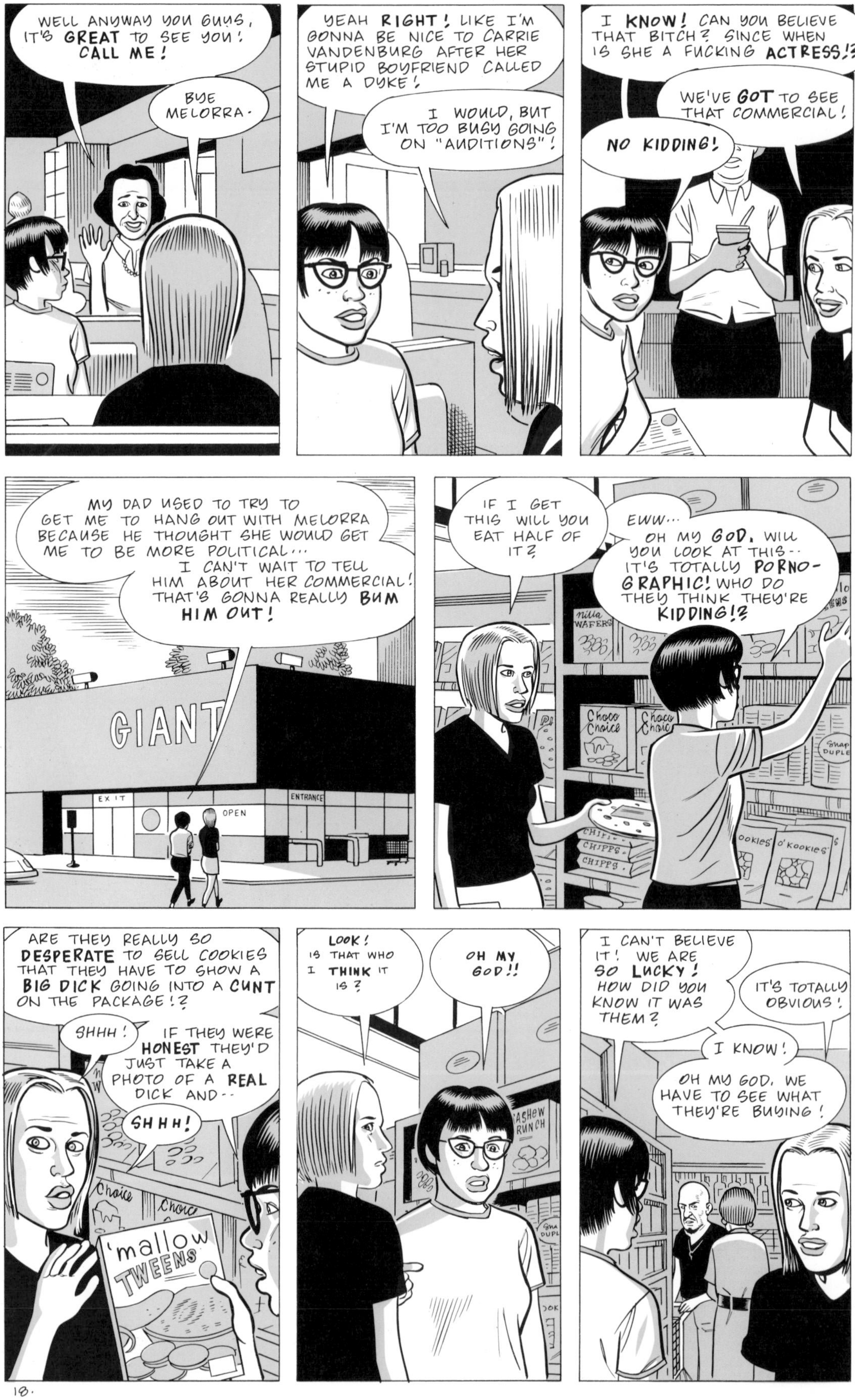
WELL ANYWAY YOU GUYS, IT'S GREAT TO SEE YOU! CALL ME!
BYE MELORRA.
YEAH RIGHT! LIKE I'M GONNA BE NICE TO CARRIE VANDENBURG AFTER HER STUPID BOYFRIEND CALLED ME A DYKE!
I WOULD, BUT I'M TOO BUSY GOING ON "AUDITIONS"!
I KNOW! CAN YOU BELIEVE THAT BITCH? SINCE WHEN IS SHE A FUCKING ACTRESS!?
WE'VE GOT TO SEE THAT COMMERCIAL!
NO KIDDING!
MY DAD USED TO TRY TO GET ME TO HANG OUT WITH MELORRA BECAUSE HE THOUGHT SHE WOULD GET ME TO BE MORE POLITICAL...
I CAN'T WAIT TO TELL HIM ABOUT HER COMMERCIAL! THAT'S GONNA REALLY BUM HIM OUT!
GIANT
EXIT
ENTRANCE
OPEN
IF I GET THIS WILL YOU EAT HALF OF IT?
EWW...
OH MY GOD, WILL YOU LOOK AT THIS -- IT'S TOTALLY PORNOGRAPHIC! WHO DO THEY THINK THEY'RE KIDDING!?
Nilla WAFERS
Choco Choice
CHIPPS
O'Kookies
ARE THEY REALLY SO DESPERATE TO SELL COOKIES THAT THEY HAVE TO SHOW A BIG DICK GOING INTO A CUNT ON THE PACKAGE!?
SHHH!
IF THEY WERE HONEST THEY'D JUST TAKE A PHOTO OF A REAL DICK AND --
SHHH!
'mallow TWEENS
LOOK! IS THAT WHO I THINK IT IS?
OH MY GOD!!
I CAN'T BELIEVE IT! WE ARE SO LUCKY! HOW DID YOU KNOW IT WAS THEM?
IT'S TOTALLY OBVIOUS!
I KNOW!
OH MY GOD, WE HAVE TO SEE WHAT THEY'RE BUYING!

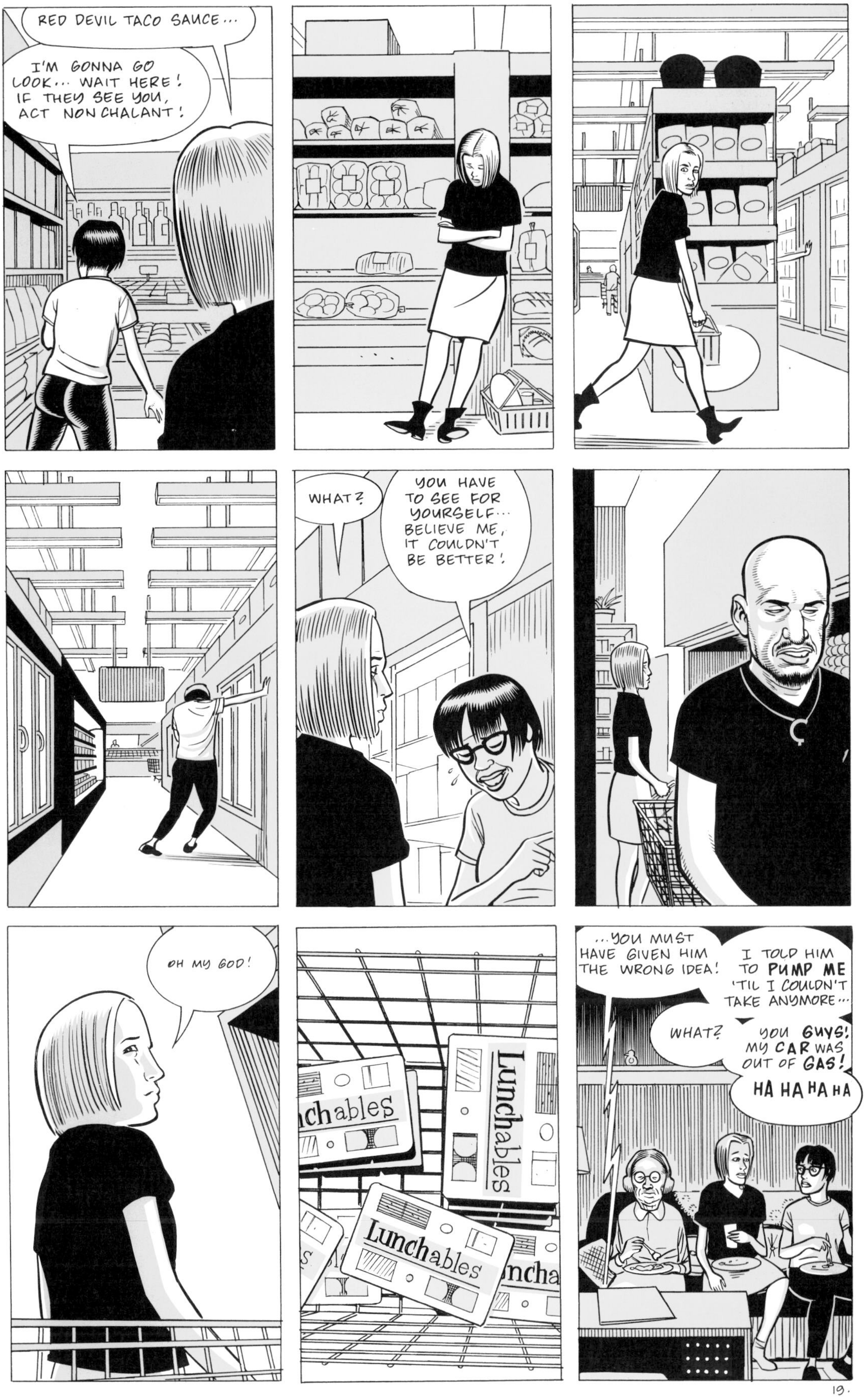
RED DEVIL TACO SAUCE...
I'M GONNA GO LOOK... WAIT HERE! IF THEY SEE YOU, ACT NONCHALANT!
WHAT?
YOU HAVE TO SEE FOR YOURSELF... BELIEVE ME, IT COULDN'T BE BETTER!
OH MY GOD!
Lunchables
Lunchables
Lunchables
...YOU MUST HAVE GIVEN HIM THE WRONG IDEA!
I TOLD HIM TO PUMP ME 'TIL I COULDN'T TAKE ANYMORE...
WHAT?
YOU GUYS! MY CAR WAS OUT OF GAS!
HA HA HA HA HA

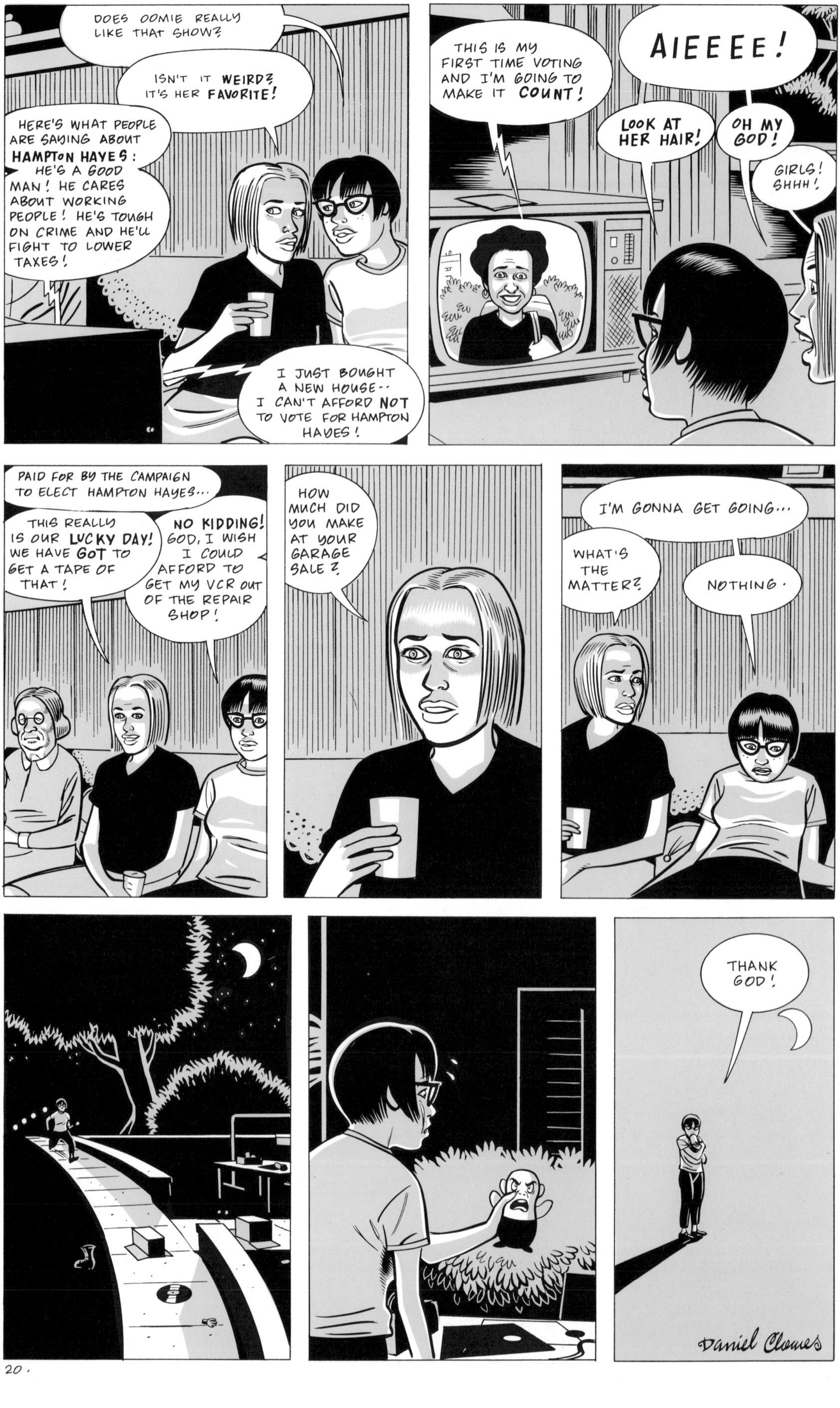
DOES OOMIE REALLY LIKE THAT SHOW?
ISN'T IT WEIRD? IT'S HER FAVORITE!
HERE'S WHAT PEOPLE ARE SAYING ABOUT HAMPTON HAYES: HE'S A GOOD MAN! HE CARES ABOUT WORKING PEOPLE! HE'S TOUGH ON CRIME AND HE'LL FIGHT TO LOWER TAXES!
I JUST BOUGHT A NEW HOUSE-- I CAN'T AFFORD NOT TO VOTE FOR HAMPTON HAYES!
THIS IS MY FIRST TIME VOTING AND I'M GOING TO MAKE IT COUNT!
AIEEEE!
LOOK AT HER HAIR!
OH MY GOD!
GIRLS! SHHH!
PAID FOR BY THE CAMPAIGN TO ELECT HAMPTON HAYES...
THIS REALLY IS OUR LUCKY DAY! WE HAVE GOT TO GET A TAPE OF THAT!
NO KIDDING! GOD, I WISH I COULD AFFORD TO GET MY VCR OUT OF THE REPAIR SHOP!
HOW MUCH DID YOU MAKE AT YOUR GARAGE SALE?
I'M GONNA GET GOING...
WHAT'S THE MATTER?
NOTHING.
THANK GOD!
Daniel Clowes

GHOST WORLD

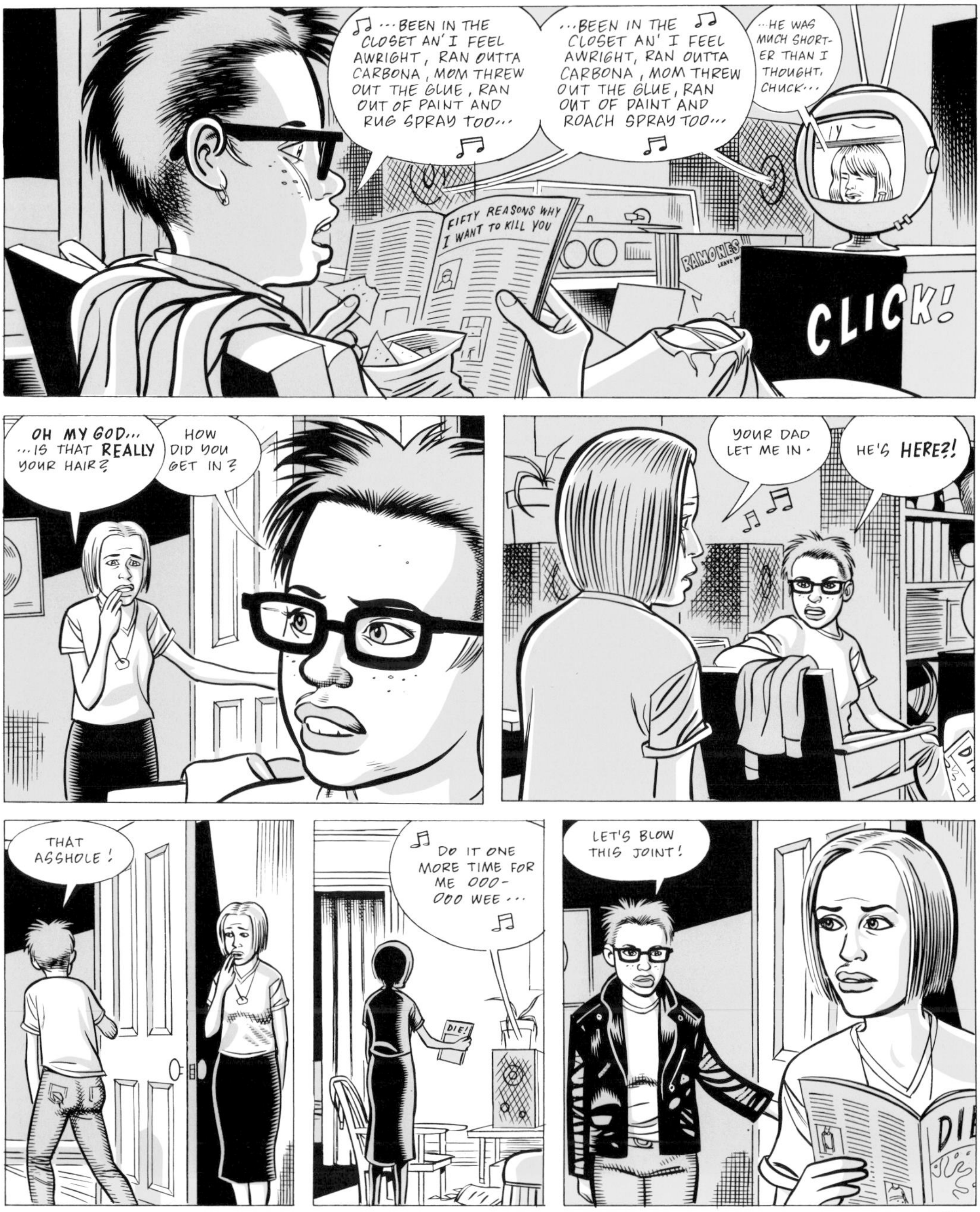
...BEEN IN THE CLOSET AN' I FEEL AWRIGHT, RAN OUTTA CARBONA, MOM THREW OUT THE GLUE, RAN OUT OF PAINT AND RUG SPRAY TOO...
...BEEN IN THE CLOSET AN' I FEEL AWRIGHT, RAN OUTTA CARBONA, MOM THREW OUT THE GLUE, RAN OUT OF PAINT AND ROACH SPRAY TOO...
...HE WAS MUCH SHORTER THAN I THOUGHT, CHUCK...
FIFTY REASONS WHY I WANT TO KILL YOU
RAMONES
CLICK!
OH MY GOD... ...IS THAT REALLY YOUR HAIR?
HOW DID YOU GET IN?
YOUR DAD LET ME IN.
HE'S HERE?!
THAT ASSHOLE!
DO IT ONE MORE TIME FOR ME OOO-OOO WEE...
DIE!
LET'S BLOW THIS JOINT!
DIE

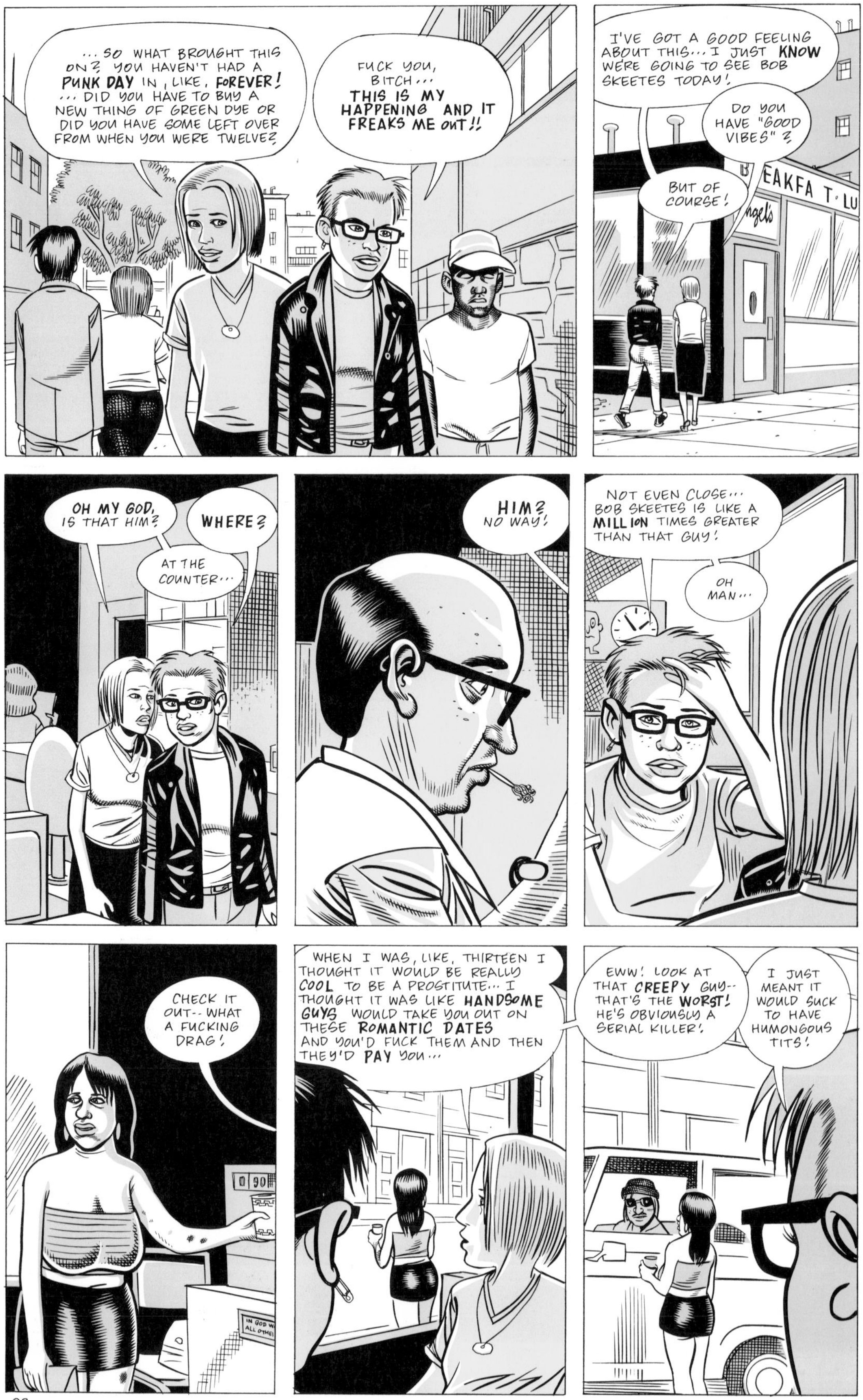
...SO WHAT BROUGHT THIS ON? YOU HAVEN'T HAD A PUNK DAY IN, LIKE, FOREVER! ...DID YOU HAVE TO BUY A NEW THING OF GREEN DYE OR DID YOU HAVE SOME LEFT OVER FROM WHEN YOU WERE TWELVE?
FUCK YOU, BITCH... THIS IS MY HAPPENING AND IT FREAKS ME OUT!!
I'VE GOT A GOOD FEELING ABOUT THIS... I JUST KNOW WE'RE GOING TO SEE BOB SKEETES TODAY!
DO YOU HAVE "GOOD VIBES"?
BUT OF COURSE!
EAKFA T LU
OH MY GOD, IS THAT HIM?
WHERE?
AT THE COUNTER...
HIM? NO WAY!
NOT EVEN CLOSE... BOB SKEETES IS LIKE A MILLION TIMES GREATER THAN THAT GUY!
OH MAN...
CHECK IT OUT-- WHAT A FUCKING DRAG!
WHEN I WAS, LIKE, THIRTEEN I THOUGHT IT WOULD BE REALLY COOL TO BE A PROSTITUTE... I THOUGHT IT WAS LIKE HANDSOME GUYS WOULD TAKE YOU OUT ON THESE ROMANTIC DATES AND YOU'D FUCK THEM AND THEN THEY'D PAY YOU...
EWW! LOOK AT THAT CREEPY GUY-- THAT'S THE WORST! HE'S OBVIOUSLY A SERIAL KILLER!
I JUST MEANT IT WOULD SUCK TO HAVE HUMONGOUS TITS!

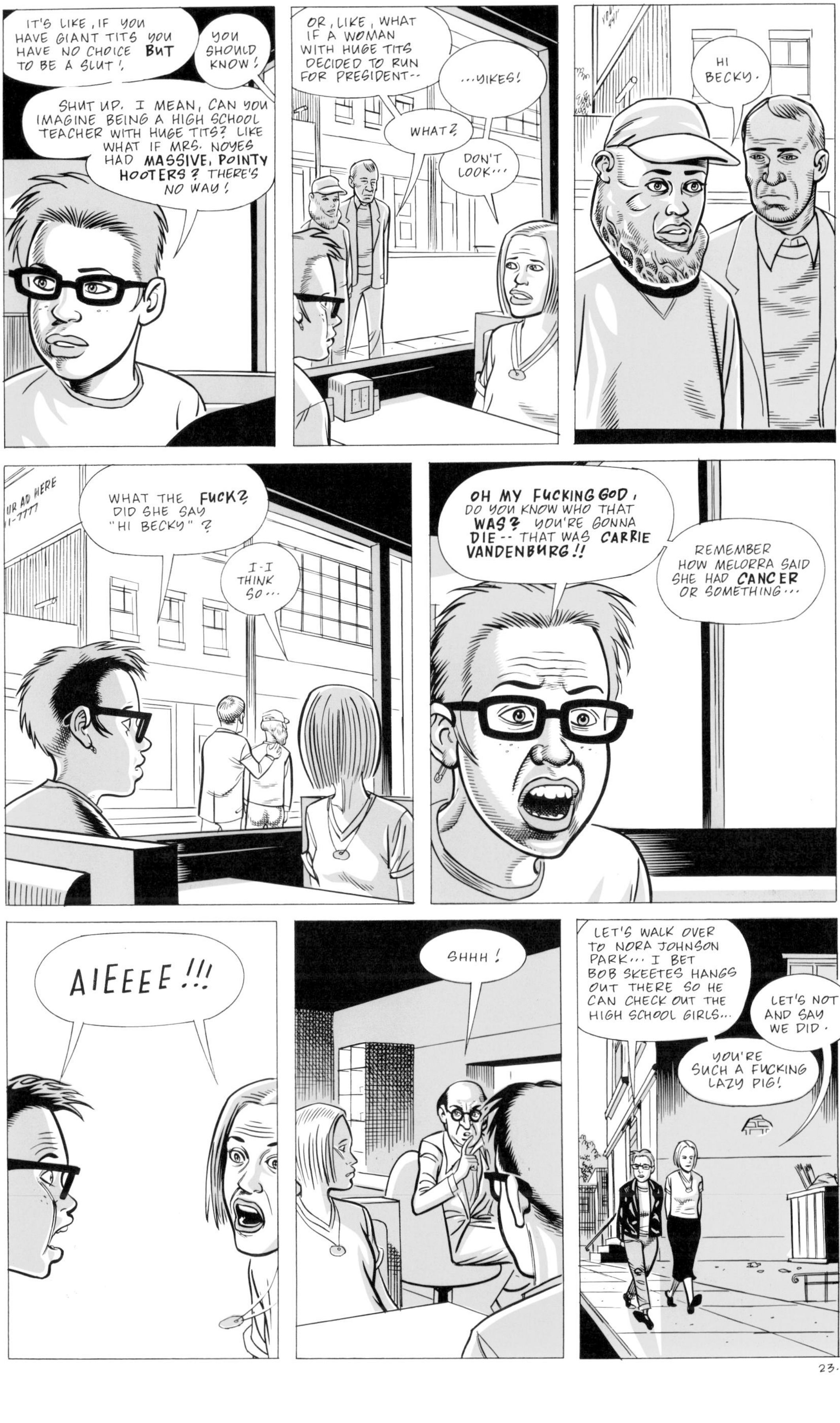
IT'S LIKE, IF YOU HAVE GIANT TITS YOU HAVE NO CHOICE BUT TO BE A SLUT!
YOU SHOULD KNOW!
SHUT UP. I MEAN, CAN YOU IMAGINE BEING A HIGH SCHOOL TEACHER WITH HUGE TITS? LIKE WHAT IF MRS. NOYES HAD MASSIVE, POINTY HOOTERS? THERE'S NO WAY!
OR, LIKE, WHAT IF A WOMAN WITH HUGE TITS DECIDED TO RUN FOR PRESIDENT--
...YIKES!
WHAT?
DON'T LOOK...
HI BECKY.
WHAT THE FUCK? DID SHE SAY "HI BECKY"?
I-I THINK SO...
OH MY FUCKING GOD, DO YOU KNOW WHO THAT WAS? YOU'RE GONNA DIE-- THAT WAS CARRIE VANDENBURG!!
REMEMBER HOW MELORRA SAID SHE HAD CANCER OR SOMETHING...
AIEEEE!!!
SHHH!
LET'S WALK OVER TO NORA JOHNSON PARK... I BET BOB SKEETES HANGS OUT THERE SO HE CAN CHECK OUT THE HIGH SCHOOL GIRLS...
LET'S NOT AND SAY WE DID.
YOU'RE SUCH A FUCKING LAZY PIG!

CHECK IT OUT-- SOMEONE LEFT THEIR HOMELESS BOARD...

HOMELESS VET # will work 2 kids THANK YOU

HEY! HEY ENID!

YEAH ??

REMEMBER ME? JOHN CROWLEY.

OH YEAH! HEY!

WHAT'S UP? ...DO YOU STILL HANG OUT AT THE CHINESE?

ED McCURDY
AUG 17

NAH... I THINK IT'S CLOSED...

IT'S JUST AS WELL... I CAN'T LISTEN TO THAT SHIT ANYMORE! I'VE BEEN GOING TO BUSINESS SCHOOL... I'M GONNA BE A BIG-ASS CORPORATE FUCK!

I'M GONNA WORK FOR TEN YEARS, FUCK THINGS UP FROM THE INSIDE AS MUCH AS I CAN, AND THEN RETIRE WHEN I'M THIRTY-FIVE!

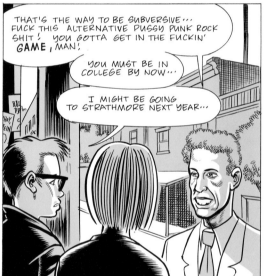

THAT'S THE WAY TO BE SUBVERSIVE... FUCK THIS ALTERNATIVE PUSSY PUNK ROCK SHIT! YOU GOTTA GET IN THE FUCKIN' GAME, MAN!

YOU MUST BE IN COLLEGE BY NOW...

I MIGHT BE GOING TO STRATHMORE NEXT YEAR...

SINCE WHEN?

I MIGHT!

IT MUST BE NICE TO HAVE EVERYTHING PAID FOR BY MOMMY AND DADDY!

I'M PAYING FOR IT MYSELF!

YEAH RIGHT... GOOD LUCK! YOU'RE GONNA BE PAYING OFF LOANS WHEN YOU'RE NINETY!

ANYWAY, I'M LATE! I GOTTA SPLIT!

FORGET ABOUT THAT PUNK ROCK SHIT-- GET OUT IN THE REAL WORLD AND MAKE SOME MONEY!

GO DIE, ASSHOLE.

WHO WAS THAT?

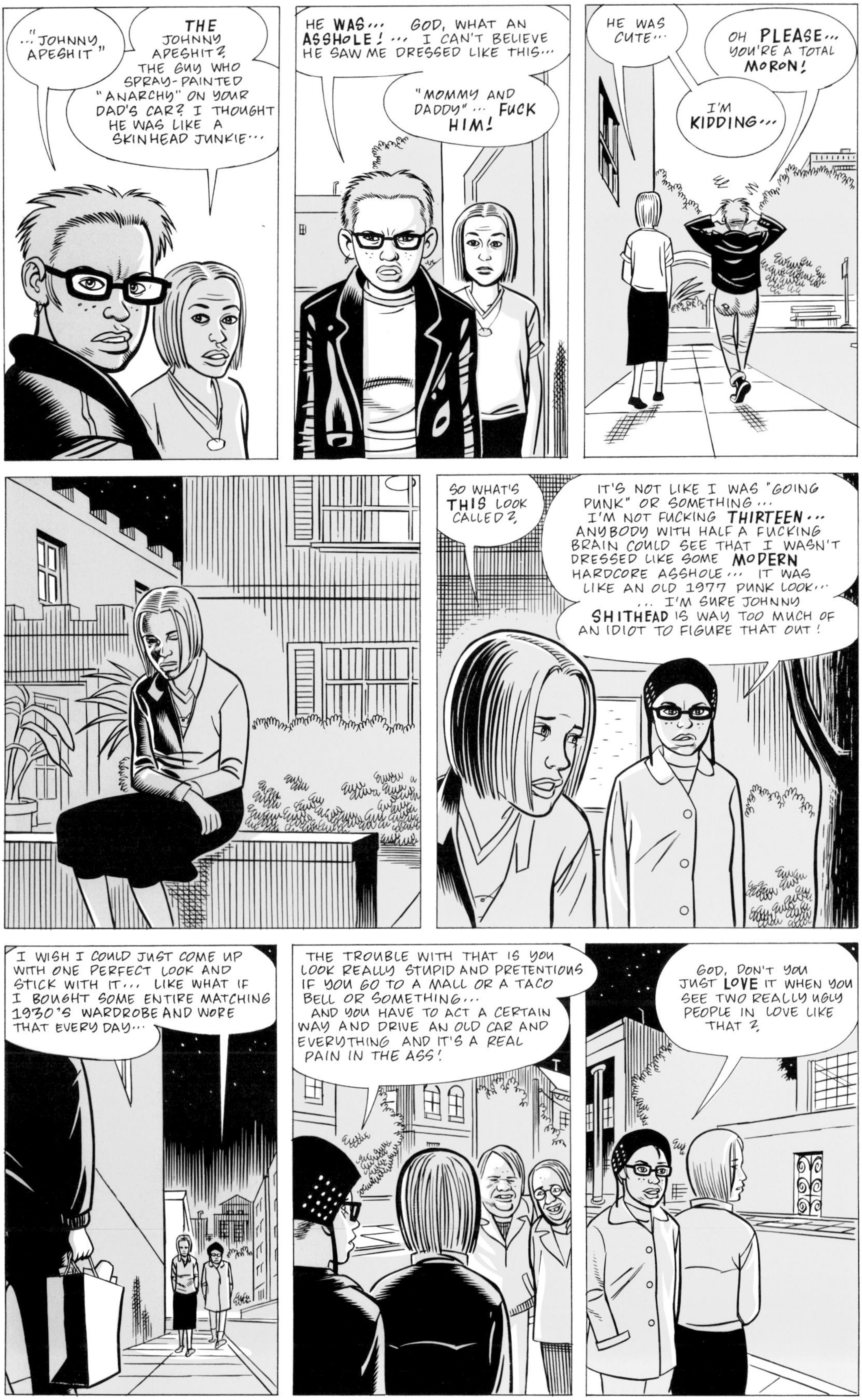
..."JOHNNY APESHIT"
THE JOHNNY APESHIT? THE GUY WHO SPRAY-PAINTED "ANARCHY" ON YOUR DAD'S CAR? I THOUGHT HE WAS LIKE A SKINHEAD JUNKIE...
HE WAS... GOD, WHAT AN ASSHOLE!... I CAN'T BELIEVE HE SAW ME DRESSED LIKE THIS...
"MOMMY AND DADDY"... FUCK HIM!
HE WAS CUTE...
OH PLEASE... YOU'RE A TOTAL MORON!
I'M KIDDING...
SO WHAT'S THIS LOOK CALLED?
IT'S NOT LIKE I WAS "GOING PUNK" OR SOMETHING... I'M NOT FUCKING THIRTEEN... ANYBODY WITH HALF A FUCKING BRAIN COULD SEE THAT I WASN'T DRESSED LIKE SOME MODERN HARDCORE ASSHOLE... IT WAS LIKE AN OLD 1977 PUNK LOOK... ... I'M SURE JOHNNY SHITHEAD IS WAY TOO MUCH OF AN IDIOT TO FIGURE THAT OUT!
I WISH I COULD JUST COME UP WITH ONE PERFECT LOOK AND STICK WITH IT... LIKE WHAT IF I BOUGHT SOME ENTIRE MATCHING 1930'S WARDROBE AND WORE THAT EVERY DAY...
THE TROUBLE WITH THAT IS YOU LOOK REALLY STUPID AND PRETENTIOUS IF YOU GO TO A MALL OR A TACO BELL OR SOMETHING... AND YOU HAVE TO ACT A CERTAIN WAY AND DRIVE AN OLD CAR AND EVERYTHING AND IT'S A REAL PAIN IN THE ASS!
GOD, DON'T YOU JUST LOVE IT WHEN YOU SEE TWO REALLY UGLY PEOPLE IN LOVE LIKE THAT?

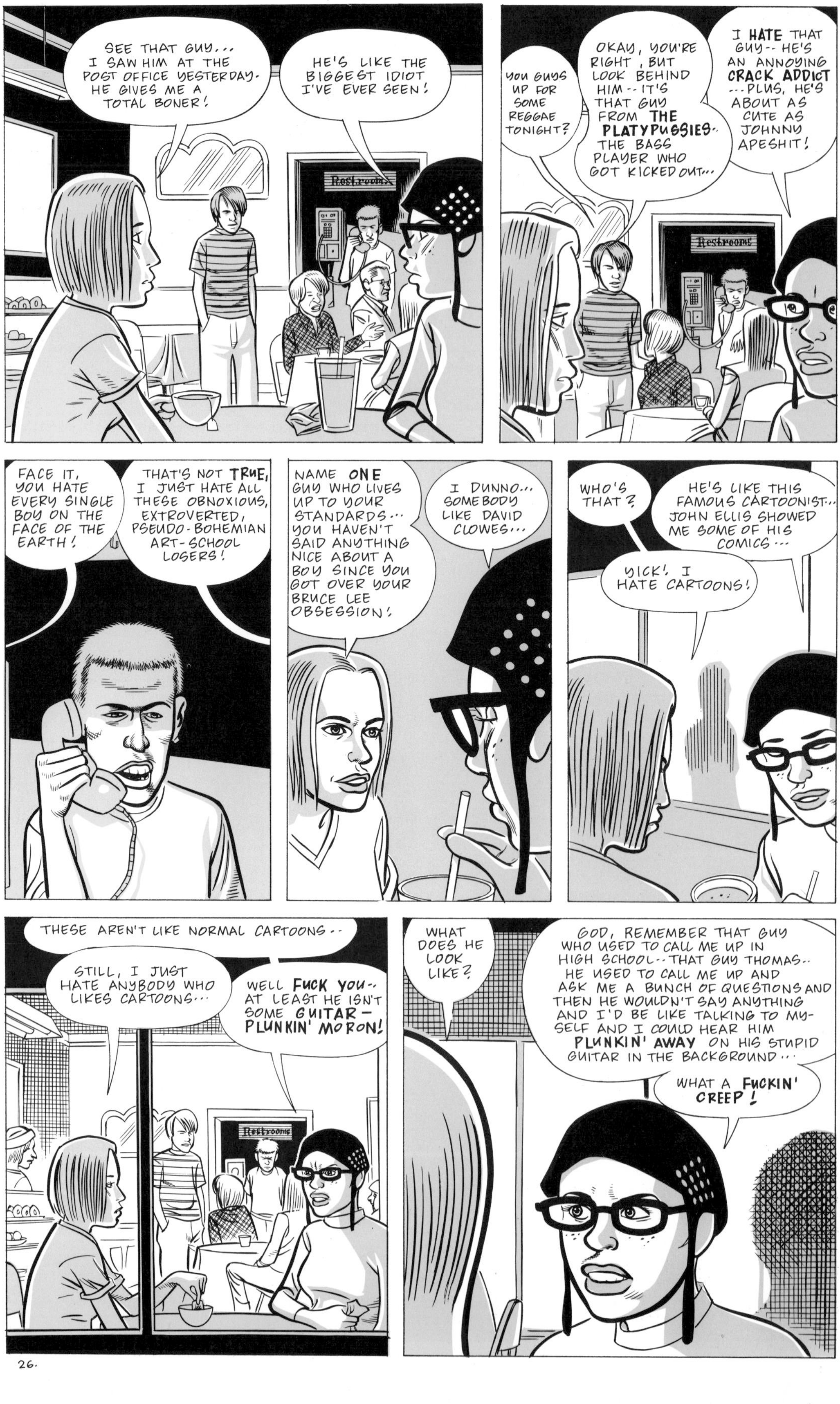

SEE THAT GUY... I SAW HIM AT THE POST OFFICE YESTERDAY. HE GIVES ME A TOTAL BONER!
HE'S LIKE THE BIGGEST IDIOT I'VE EVER SEEN!
Restrooms
YOU GUYS UP FOR SOME REGGAE TONIGHT?
OKAY, YOU'RE RIGHT, BUT LOOK BEHIND HIM -- IT'S THAT GUY FROM THE PLATYPUSSIES. THE BASS PLAYER WHO GOT KICKED OUT...
I HATE THAT GUY -- HE'S AN ANNOYING CRACK ADDICT ... PLUS, HE'S ABOUT AS CUTE AS JOHNNY APESHIT!
Restrooms
FACE IT, YOU HATE EVERY SINGLE BOY ON THE FACE OF THE EARTH!
THAT'S NOT TRUE, I JUST HATE ALL THESE OBNOXIOUS, EXTROVERTED, PSEUDO-BOHEMIAN ART-SCHOOL LOSERS!
NAME ONE GUY WHO LIVES UP TO YOUR STANDARDS... YOU HAVEN'T SAID ANYTHING NICE ABOUT A BOY SINCE YOU GOT OVER YOUR BRUCE LEE OBSESSION!
I DUNNO... SOMEBODY LIKE DAVID CLOWES...
WHO'S THAT?
HE'S LIKE THIS FAMOUS CARTOONIST... JOHN ELLIS SHOWED ME SOME OF HIS COMICS...
YICK! I HATE CARTOONS!
THESE AREN'T LIKE NORMAL CARTOONS --
STILL, I JUST HATE ANYBODY WHO LIKES CARTOONS...
WELL FUCK YOU -- AT LEAST HE ISN'T SOME GUITAR-PLUNKIN' MORON!
Restrooms
WHAT DOES HE LOOK LIKE?
GOD, REMEMBER THAT GUY WHO USED TO CALL ME UP IN HIGH SCHOOL -- THAT GUY THOMAS -- HE USED TO CALL ME UP AND ASK ME A BUNCH OF QUESTIONS AND THEN HE WOULDN'T SAY ANYTHING AND I'D BE LIKE TALKING TO MYSELF AND I COULD HEAR HIM PLUNKIN' AWAY ON HIS STUPID GUITAR IN THE BACKGROUND...
WHAT A FUCKIN' CREEP!

HE LOOKS LIKE **HIM**?

NO... I CHANGED THE SUBJECT TO GUITAR-PLUNKIN' MORONS. I ALSO THINK HE USED TO ASK ME QUESTIONS SO HE COULD JERK OFF TO THE SOUND OF MY VOICE!

WELL, LOOK WHO'S HERE... **SHALOM!**

FUCK YOU! SINCE WHEN DO YOU WORK HERE?

ZINE·O·PHOBIA

FOR REN

SINCE ALWAYS ON TUESDAY... **HI REBECCA**...

SHE'S PRETENDING SHE CAN'T HEAR YOU.

PENUS #2

THE MONKS + THE THREE GUNS

SHE THINKS SHE'S CUTE ENOUGH TO PULL OFF THAT *STUCK-UP VIRGIN ICE-QUEEN* SHTICK...

SHE IS.

I GUESS YOU WOULD KNOW!

HEY, SPEAKING OF LESBIANS, I JUST GOT THIS **INCREDIBLE** VIDEOTAPE FROM SOME GUY IN **MANITOBA**... IT'S LIKE A TENTH GENERATION DUB OF THESE TWO CANADIAN **BULL DYKES** DRUNKENLY **TORTURING** SOME HIGH SCHOOL JOCK IN THIS **ABANDONED SCHOOLHOUSE**...

MMM...

ZINE·O·PHOBIA SPECIAL APPEARANCES

JULY 3 CANCELLED
5 MR. + MRS. DOG SHIT
6 DR. DEATH   ZINE
10 DAN CLOWES - COMICS
11 HARVEY SID FISHER
14 SKIN GRAFT
ORE TAMMY - WIGLET
MILT

...IT'S REALLY HARD TO SEE BUT THERE'S THIS PART WHERE IT LOOKS LIKE THEY **PEEL AWAY** THE SKIN ON HIS FINGERS AND **SCRAPE** HIS **BONY STUMPS** ACROSS THE **BLACKBOARD!**

TY GE
MASS MURDERER CARDS
JEFFERY DAHME CARD

WHAT DID JOHN ELLIS SAY ABOUT ME?

HE LOVES YOU... IT'S SO PATHETIC...

HEY **LOOK!** IT'S THE **PANTS!**

I CAN'T BELIEVE THEY'RE STILL HERE!

YOU LOOK LIKE EDDIE MUNSTER...

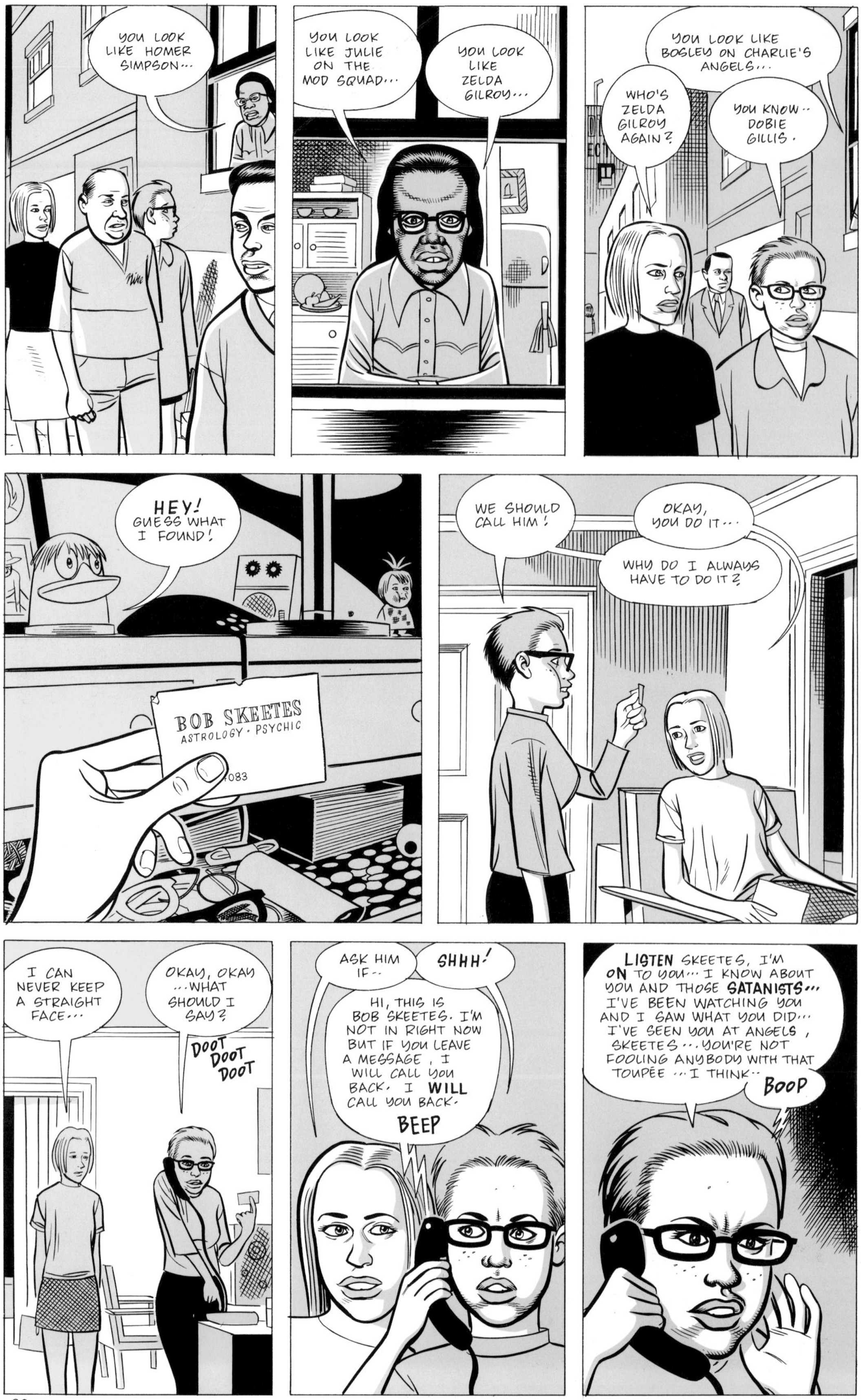
YOU LOOK LIKE HOMER SIMPSON...
YOU LOOK LIKE JULIE ON THE MOD SQUAD...
YOU LOOK LIKE ZELDA GILROY...
YOU LOOK LIKE BOSLEY ON CHARLIE'S ANGELS...
WHO'S ZELDA GILROY AGAIN?
YOU KNOW.. DOBIE GILLIS.
HEY! GUESS WHAT I FOUND!
BOB SKEETES
ASTROLOGY • PSYCHIC
WE SHOULD CALL HIM!
OKAY, YOU DO IT...
WHY DO I ALWAYS HAVE TO DO IT?
I CAN NEVER KEEP A STRAIGHT FACE...
OKAY, OKAY ...WHAT SHOULD I SAY?
DOOT DOOT DOOT
ASK HIM IF--
SHHH!
HI, THIS IS BOB SKEETES. I'M NOT IN RIGHT NOW BUT IF YOU LEAVE A MESSAGE, I WILL CALL YOU BACK. I WILL CALL YOU BACK.
BEEP
LISTEN SKEETES, I'M ON TO YOU... I KNOW ABOUT YOU AND THOSE SATANISTS... I'VE BEEN WATCHING YOU AND I SAW WHAT YOU DID... I'VE SEEN YOU AT ANGELS, SKEETES...YOU'RE NOT FOOLING ANYBODY WITH THAT TOUPÉE ...I THINK--
BOOP

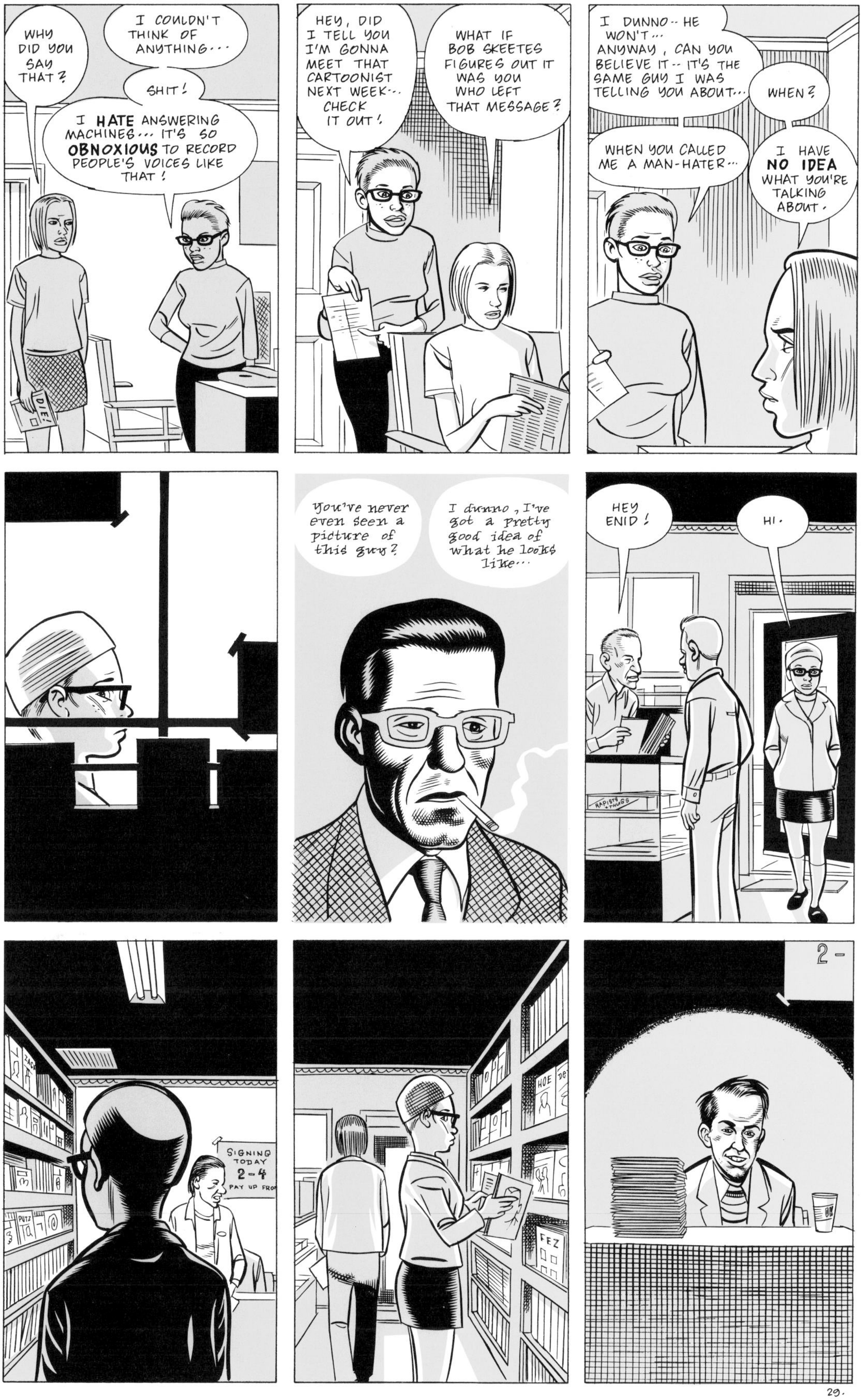
WHY DID YOU SAY THAT?
I COULDN'T THINK OF ANYTHING...
SHIT!
I HATE ANSWERING MACHINES... IT'S SO OBNOXIOUS TO RECORD PEOPLE'S VOICES LIKE THAT!
DIE!
HEY, DID I TELL YOU I'M GONNA MEET THAT CARTOONIST NEXT WEEK... CHECK IT OUT!
WHAT IF BOB SKEETES FIGURES OUT IT WAS YOU WHO LEFT THAT MESSAGE?
I DUNNO -- HE WON'T... ANYWAY, CAN YOU BELIEVE IT -- IT'S THE SAME GUY I WAS TELLING YOU ABOUT...
WHEN?
WHEN YOU CALLED ME A MAN-HATER...
I HAVE NO IDEA WHAT YOU'RE TALKING ABOUT.
You've never even seen a picture of this guy?
I dunno, I've got a pretty good idea of what he looks like...
HEY ENID!
HI.
SIGNING TODAY 2-4
PUTZ
HOE
FEZ
2-

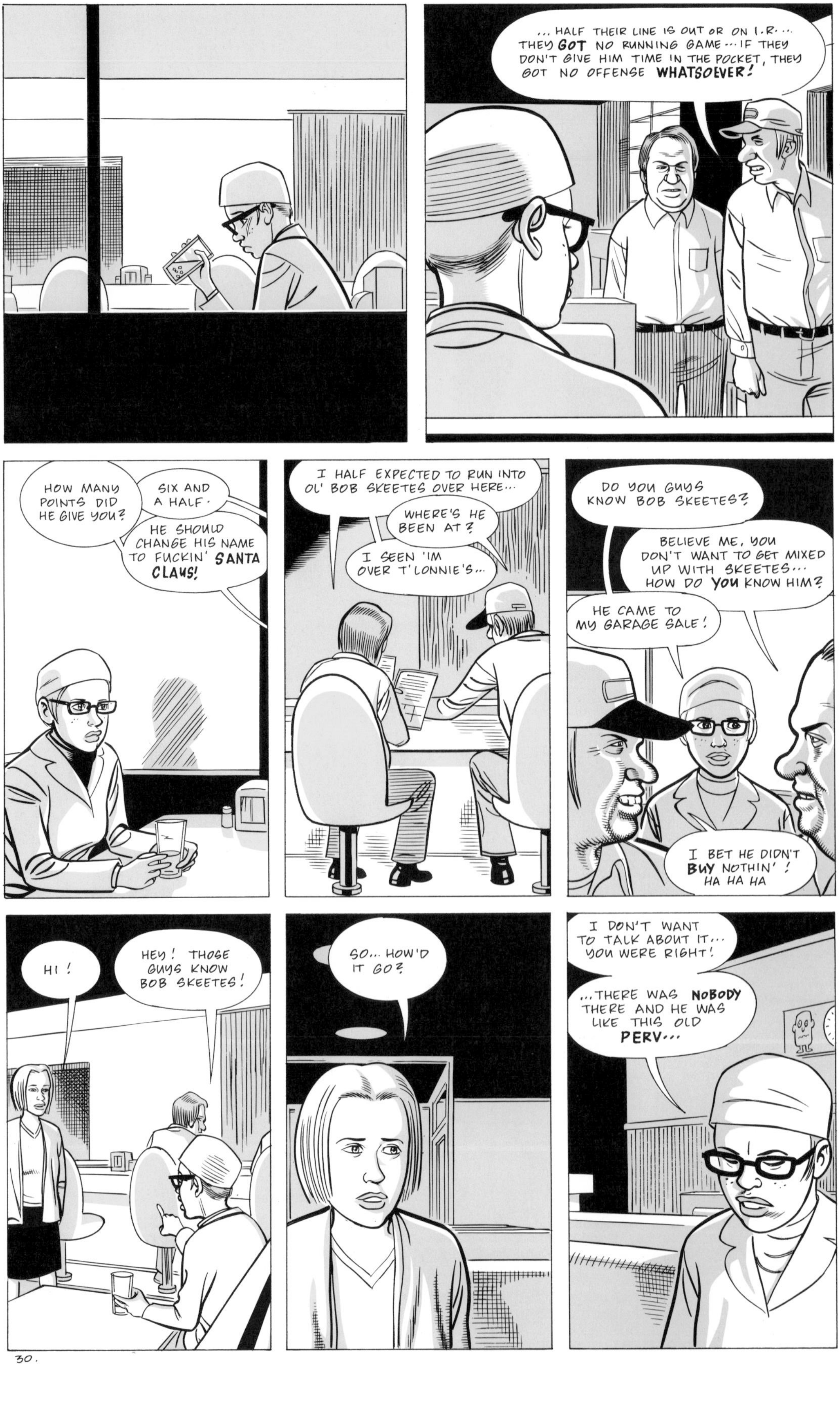
... HALF THEIR LINE IS OUT OR ON I.R. ... THEY GOT NO RUNNING GAME ... IF THEY DON'T GIVE HIM TIME IN THE POCKET, THEY GOT NO OFFENSE WHATSOEVER!
HOW MANY POINTS DID HE GIVE YOU?
SIX AND A HALF.
HE SHOULD CHANGE HIS NAME TO FUCKIN' SANTA CLAUS!
I HALF EXPECTED TO RUN INTO OL' BOB SKEETES OVER HERE...
WHERE'S HE BEEN AT?
I SEEN 'IM OVER T'LONNIE'S...
DO YOU GUYS KNOW BOB SKEETES?
BELIEVE ME, YOU DON'T WANT TO GET MIXED UP WITH SKEETES... HOW DO YOU KNOW HIM?
HE CAME TO MY GARAGE SALE!
I BET HE DIDN'T BUY NOTHIN'! HA HA HA
HI!
HEY! THOSE GUYS KNOW BOB SKEETES!
SO... HOW'D IT GO?
I DON'T WANT TO TALK ABOUT IT... YOU WERE RIGHT!
...THERE WAS NOBODY THERE AND HE WAS LIKE THIS OLD PERV...

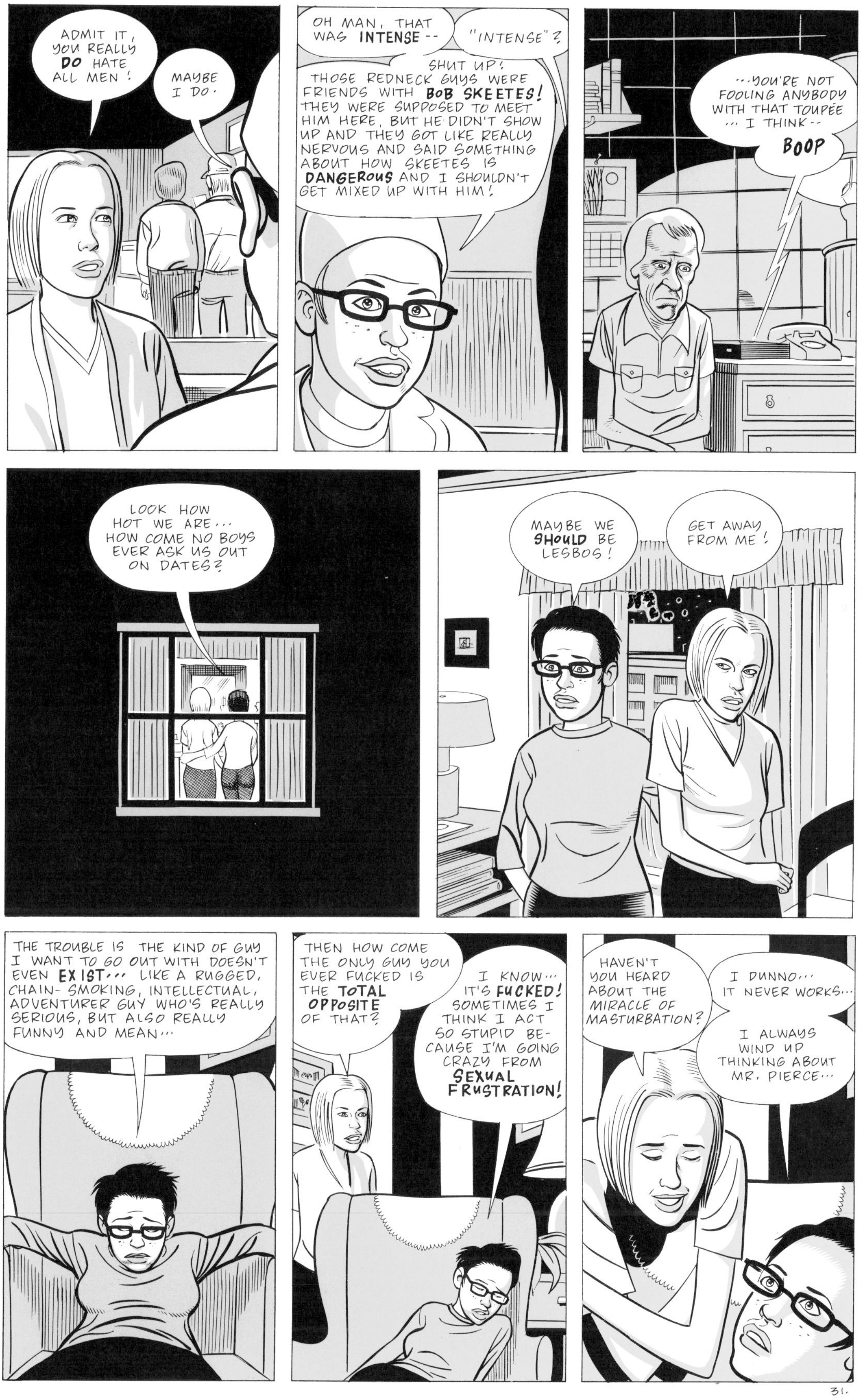
ADMIT IT, YOU REALLY DO HATE ALL MEN!
MAYBE I DO.
OH MAN, THAT WAS INTENSE --
"INTENSE"?
SHUT UP! THOSE REDNECK GUYS WERE FRIENDS WITH BOB SKEETES! THEY WERE SUPPOSED TO MEET HIM HERE, BUT HE DIDN'T SHOW UP AND THEY GOT LIKE REALLY NERVOUS AND SAID SOMETHING ABOUT HOW SKEETES IS DANGEROUS AND I SHOULDN'T GET MIXED UP WITH HIM!
...YOU'RE NOT FOOLING ANYBODY WITH THAT TOUPÉE ... I THINK --
BOOP
LOOK HOW HOT WE ARE... HOW COME NO BOYS EVER ASK US OUT ON DATES?
MAYBE WE SHOULD BE LESBOS!
GET AWAY FROM ME!
THE TROUBLE IS THE KIND OF GUY I WANT TO GO OUT WITH DOESN'T EVEN EXIST... LIKE A RUGGED, CHAIN-SMOKING, INTELLECTUAL, ADVENTURER GUY WHO'S REALLY SERIOUS, BUT ALSO REALLY FUNNY AND MEAN...
THEN HOW COME THE ONLY GUY YOU EVER FUCKED IS THE TOTAL OPPOSITE OF THAT?
I KNOW... IT'S FUCKED! SOMETIMES I THINK I ACT SO STUPID BE-CAUSE I'M GOING CRAZY FROM SEXUAL FRUSTRATION!
HAVEN'T YOU HEARD ABOUT THE MIRACLE OF MASTURBATION?
I DUNNO... IT NEVER WORKS...
I ALWAYS WIND UP THINKING ABOUT MR. PIERCE...

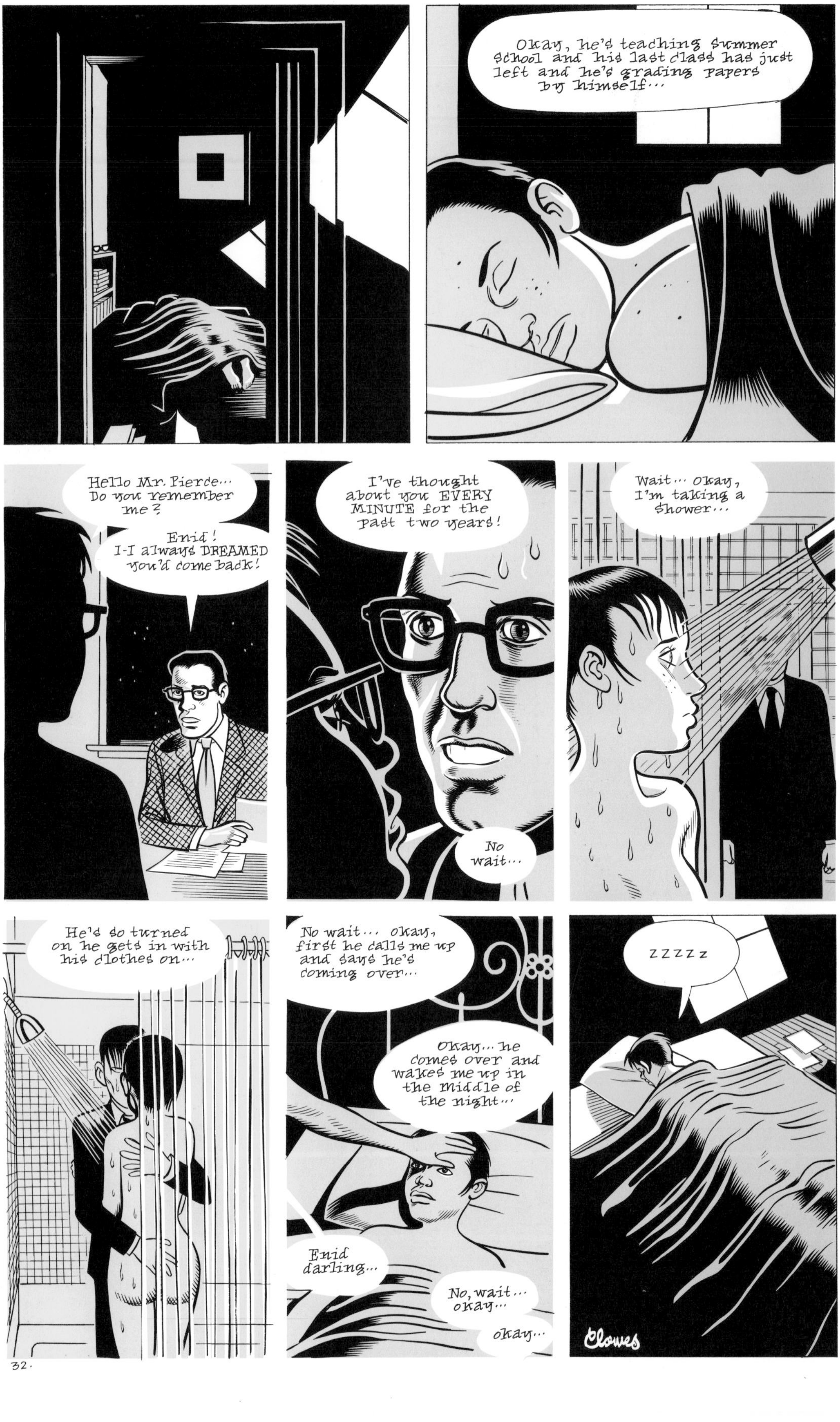
Okay, he's teaching summer school and his last class has just left and he's grading papers by himself...
Hello Mr. Pierce... Do you remember me?
Enid! I-I always DREAMED you'd come back!
I've thought about you EVERY MINUTE for the past two years!
No wait...
Wait... okay, I'm taking a shower...
He's so turned on he gets in with his clothes on...
No wait... okay, first he calls me up and says he's coming over...
Okay... he comes over and wakes me up in the middle of the night...
Enid darling...
No, wait... okay...
okay...
ZZZZZ
Clowes

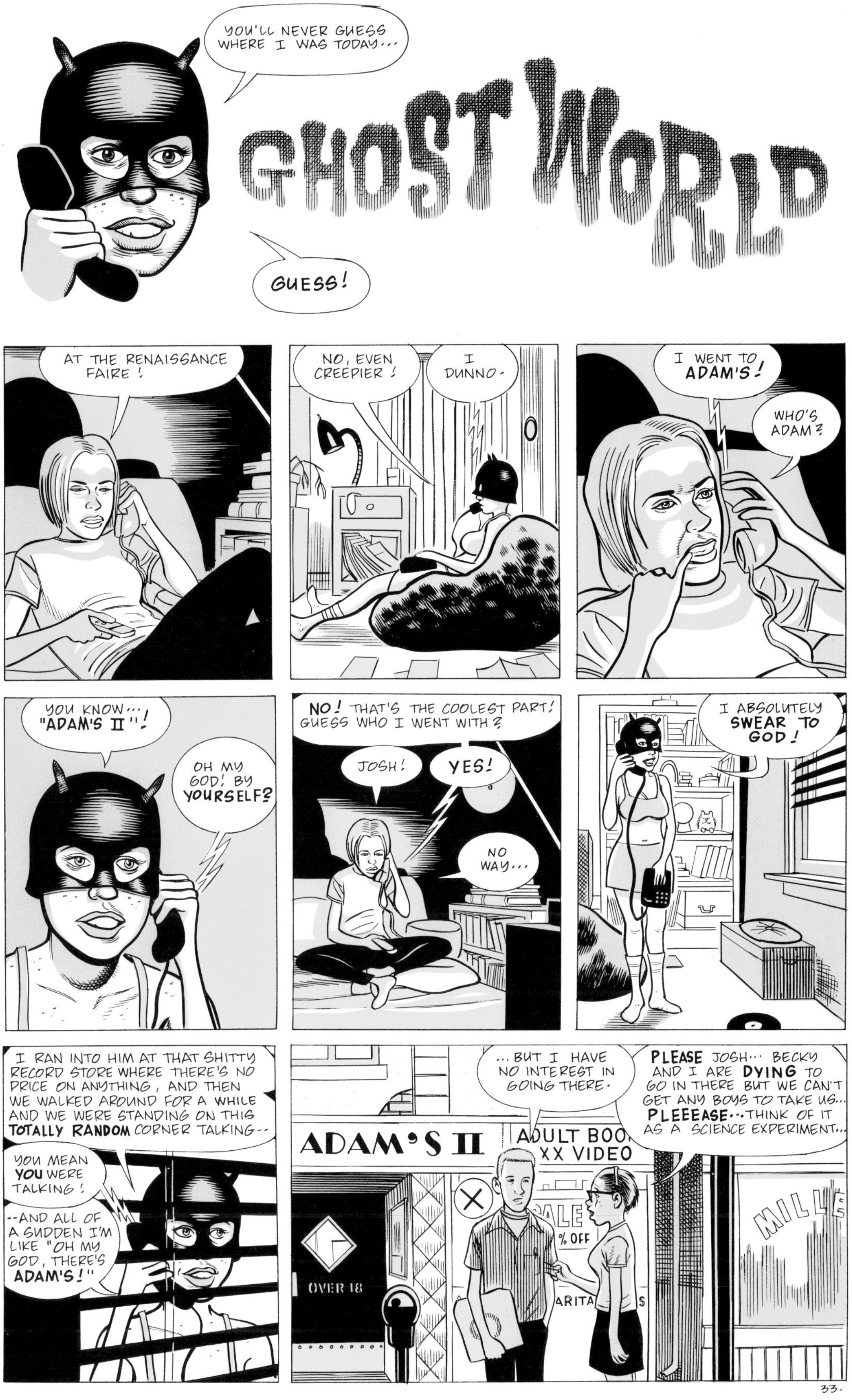
YOU'LL NEVER GUESS WHERE I WAS TODAY...
GHOST WORLD
GUESS!
AT THE RENAISSANCE FAIRE!
NO, EVEN CREEPIER!
I DUNNO.
I WENT TO ADAM'S!
WHO'S ADAM?
YOU KNOW... "ADAM'S II"!
OH MY GOD! BY YOURSELF?
NO! THAT'S THE COOLEST PART! GUESS WHO I WENT WITH?
JOSH!
YES!
NO WAY...
I ABSOLUTELY SWEAR TO GOD!
I RAN INTO HIM AT THAT SHITTY RECORD STORE WHERE THERE'S NO PRICE ON ANYTHING, AND THEN WE WALKED AROUND FOR A WHILE AND WE WERE STANDING ON THIS TOTALLY RANDOM CORNER TALKING--
YOU MEAN YOU WERE TALKING!
--AND ALL OF A SUDDEN I'M LIKE "OH MY GOD, THERE'S ADAM'S!"
...BUT I HAVE NO INTEREST IN GOING THERE.
PLEASE JOSH... BECKY AND I ARE DYING TO GO IN THERE BUT WE CAN'T GET ANY BOYS TO TAKE US... PLEEEASE... THINK OF IT AS A SCIENCE EXPERIMENT...
ADAM'S II
OVER 18
ADULT BOO
XX VIDEO
% OFF

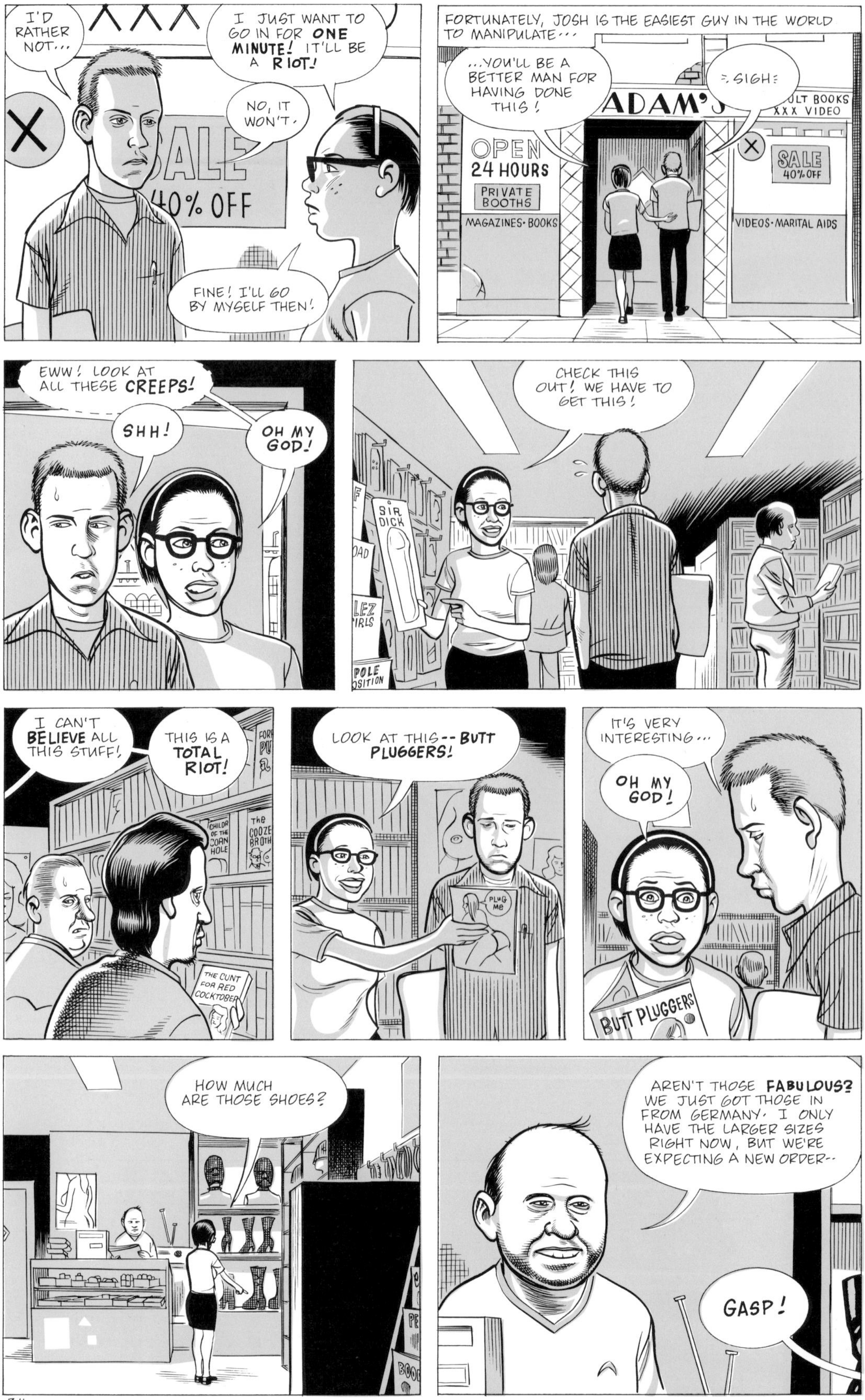

I'D RATHER NOT...
I JUST WANT TO GO IN FOR ONE MINUTE! IT'LL BE A RIOT!
NO, IT WON'T.
SALE
40% OFF
FINE! I'LL GO BY MYSELF THEN!
FORTUNATELY, JOSH IS THE EASIEST GUY IN THE WORLD TO MANIPULATE...
...YOU'LL BE A BETTER MAN FOR HAVING DONE THIS!
SIGH
ADAM'S
XXX VIDEO
OPEN
24 HOURS
PRIVATE BOOTHS
MAGAZINES · BOOKS
SALE
40% OFF
VIDEOS · MARITAL AIDS
EWW! LOOK AT ALL THESE CREEPS!
SHH!
OH MY GOD!
CHECK THIS OUT! WE HAVE TO GET THIS!
SIR DICK
I CAN'T BELIEVE ALL THIS STUFF!
THIS IS A TOTAL RIOT!
CHILDREN OF THE CORN HOLE
THE CUNT FOR RED COCKTOBER
LOOK AT THIS-- BUTT PLUGGERS!
PLUG ME
IT'S VERY INTERESTING...
OH MY GOD!
BUTT PLUGGERS
HOW MUCH ARE THOSE SHOES?
AREN'T THOSE FABULOUS? WE JUST GOT THOSE IN FROM GERMANY. I ONLY HAVE THE LARGER SIZES RIGHT NOW, BUT WE'RE EXPECTING A NEW ORDER--
GASP!

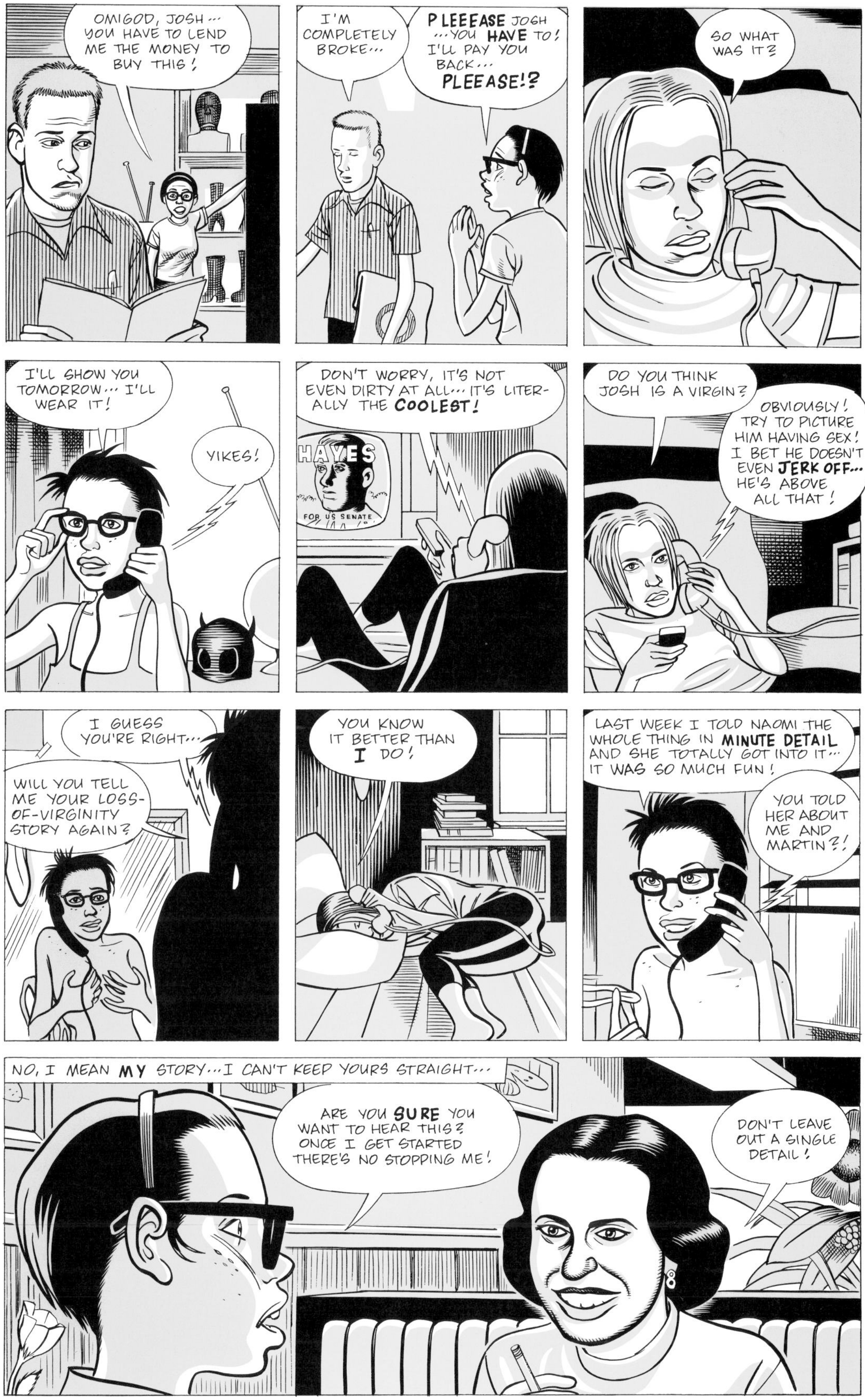
OMIGOD, JOSH... YOU HAVE TO LEND ME THE MONEY TO BUY THIS!
I'M COMPLETELY BROKE...
PLEEEASE JOSH ...YOU HAVE TO! I'LL PAY YOU BACK... PLEEASE!?
SO WHAT WAS IT?
I'LL SHOW YOU TOMORROW... I'LL WEAR IT!
YIKES!
DON'T WORRY, IT'S NOT EVEN DIRTY AT ALL... IT'S LITERALLY THE COOLEST!
HAYES
FOR US SENATE
DO YOU THINK JOSH IS A VIRGIN?
OBVIOUSLY! TRY TO PICTURE HIM HAVING SEX! I BET HE DOESN'T EVEN JERK OFF... HE'S ABOVE ALL THAT!
I GUESS YOU'RE RIGHT...
WILL YOU TELL ME YOUR LOSS-OF-VIRGINITY STORY AGAIN?
YOU KNOW IT BETTER THAN I DO!
LAST WEEK I TOLD NAOMI THE WHOLE THING IN MINUTE DETAIL AND SHE TOTALLY GOT INTO IT... IT WAS SO MUCH FUN!
YOU TOLD HER ABOUT ME AND MARTIN?!
NO, I MEAN MY STORY... I CAN'T KEEP YOURS STRAIGHT...
ARE YOU SURE YOU WANT TO HEAR THIS? ONCE I GET STARTED THERE'S NO STOPPING ME!
DON'T LEAVE OUT A SINGLE DETAIL!

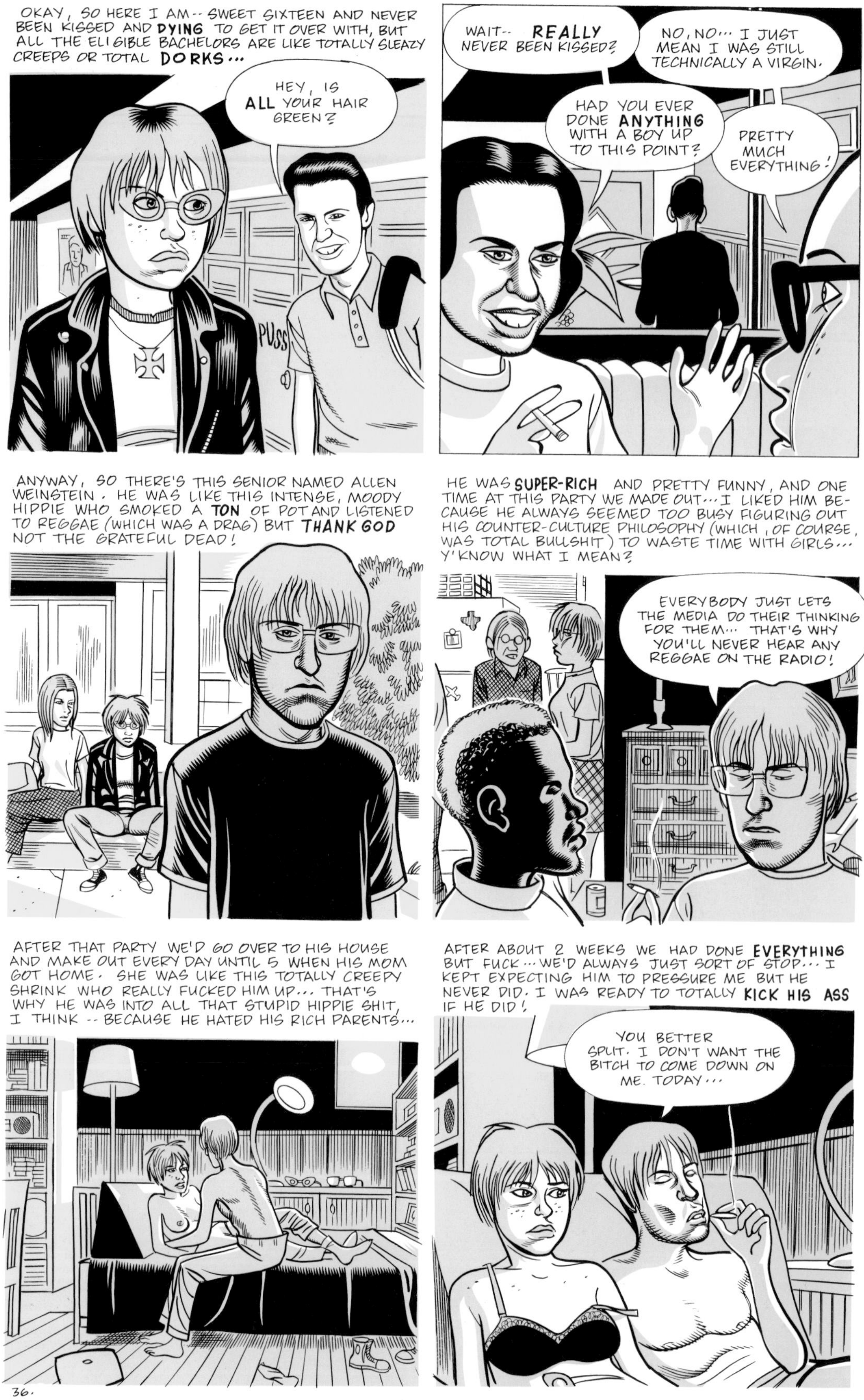
OKAY, SO HERE I AM -- SWEET SIXTEEN AND NEVER BEEN KISSED AND DYING TO GET IT OVER WITH, BUT ALL THE ELIGIBLE BACHELORS ARE LIKE TOTALLY SLEAZY CREEPS OR TOTAL DORKS...
HEY, IS ALL YOUR HAIR GREEN?
PUSS
WAIT-- REALLY NEVER BEEN KISSED?
NO, NO... I JUST MEAN I WAS STILL TECHNICALLY A VIRGIN.
HAD YOU EVER DONE ANYTHING WITH A BOY UP TO THIS POINT?
PRETTY MUCH EVERYTHING!
ANYWAY, SO THERE'S THIS SENIOR NAMED ALLEN WEINSTEIN. HE WAS LIKE THIS INTENSE, MOODY HIPPIE WHO SMOKED A TON OF POT AND LISTENED TO REGGAE (WHICH WAS A DRAG) BUT THANK GOD NOT THE GRATEFUL DEAD!
HE WAS SUPER-RICH AND PRETTY FUNNY, AND ONE TIME AT THIS PARTY WE MADE OUT... I LIKED HIM BECAUSE HE ALWAYS SEEMED TOO BUSY FIGURING OUT HIS COUNTER-CULTURE PHILOSOPHY (WHICH, OF COURSE, WAS TOTAL BULLSHIT) TO WASTE TIME WITH GIRLS... Y'KNOW WHAT I MEAN?
EVERYBODY JUST LETS THE MEDIA DO THEIR THINKING FOR THEM... THAT'S WHY YOU'LL NEVER HEAR ANY REGGAE ON THE RADIO!
AFTER THAT PARTY WE'D GO OVER TO HIS HOUSE AND MAKE OUT EVERY DAY UNTIL 5 WHEN HIS MOM GOT HOME. SHE WAS LIKE THIS TOTALLY CREEPY SHRINK WHO REALLY FUCKED HIM UP... THAT'S WHY HE WAS INTO ALL THAT STUPID HIPPIE SHIT, I THINK -- BECAUSE HE HATED HIS RICH PARENTS...
AFTER ABOUT 2 WEEKS WE HAD DONE EVERYTHING BUT FUCK... WE'D ALWAYS JUST SORT OF STOP... I KEPT EXPECTING HIM TO PRESSURE ME BUT HE NEVER DID. I WAS READY TO TOTALLY KICK HIS ASS IF HE DID!
YOU BETTER SPLIT. I DON'T WANT THE BITCH TO COME DOWN ON ME. TODAY...

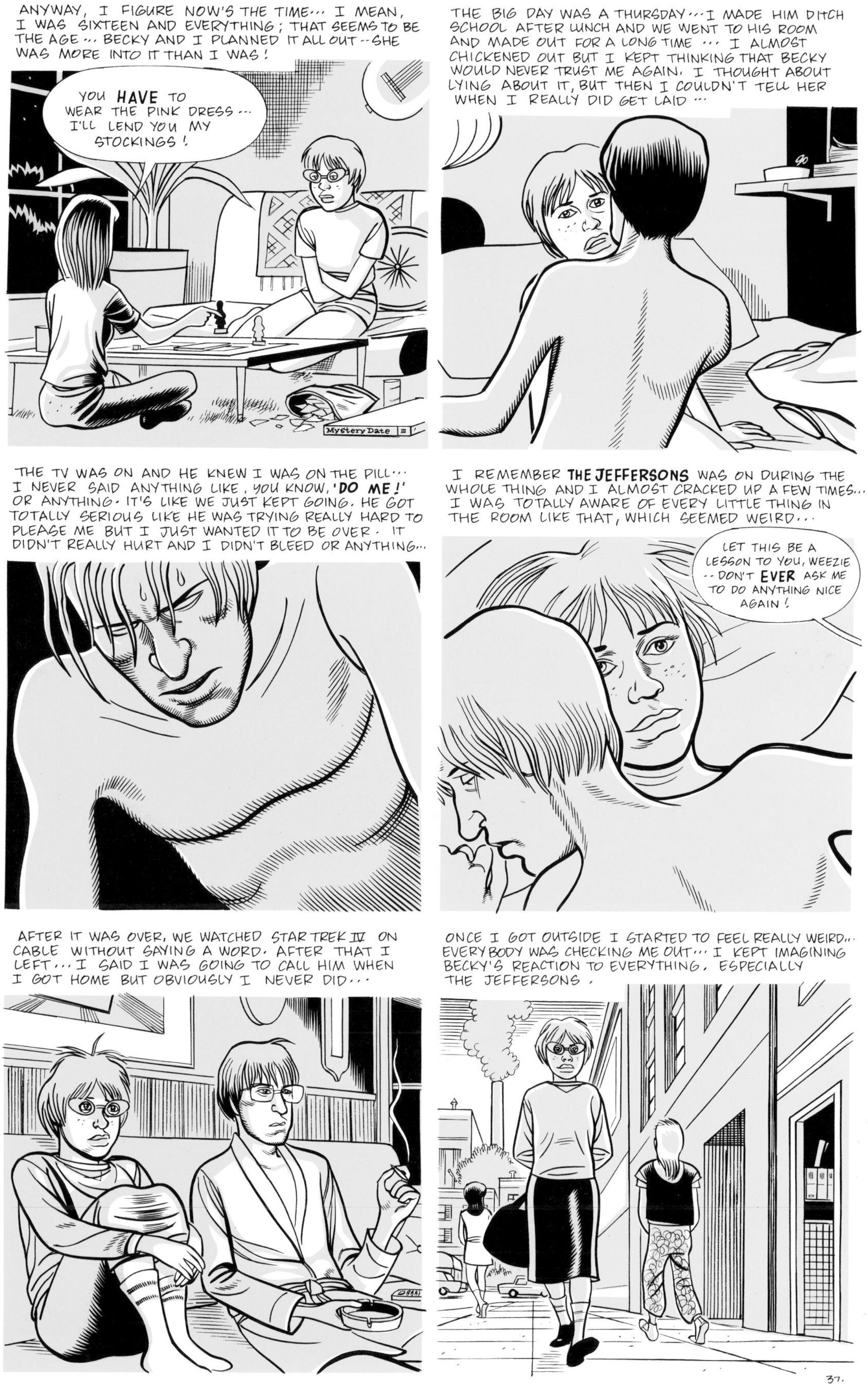
ANYWAY, I FIGURE NOW'S THE TIME... I MEAN, I WAS SIXTEEN AND EVERYTHING; THAT SEEMS TO BE THE AGE... BECKY AND I PLANNED IT ALL OUT -- SHE WAS MORE INTO IT THAN I WAS!
YOU **HAVE** TO WEAR THE PINK DRESS... I'LL LEND YOU MY STOCKINGS!
Mystery Date
THE BIG DAY WAS A THURSDAY... I MADE HIM DITCH SCHOOL AFTER LUNCH AND WE WENT TO HIS ROOM AND MADE OUT FOR A LONG TIME ... I ALMOST CHICKENED OUT BUT I KEPT THINKING THAT BECKY WOULD NEVER TRUST ME AGAIN. I THOUGHT ABOUT LYING ABOUT IT, BUT THEN I COULDN'T TELL HER WHEN I REALLY DID GET LAID ...
THE TV WAS ON AND HE KNEW I WAS ON THE PILL... I NEVER SAID ANYTHING LIKE, YOU KNOW, **'DO ME!'** OR ANYTHING. IT'S LIKE WE JUST KEPT GOING. HE GOT TOTALLY SERIOUS LIKE HE WAS TRYING REALLY HARD TO PLEASE ME BUT I JUST WANTED IT TO BE OVER. IT DIDN'T REALLY HURT AND I DIDN'T BLEED OR ANYTHING...
I REMEMBER **THE JEFFERSONS** WAS ON DURING THE WHOLE THING AND I ALMOST CRACKED UP A FEW TIMES... I WAS TOTALLY AWARE OF EVERY LITTLE THING IN THE ROOM LIKE THAT, WHICH SEEMED WEIRD...
LET THIS BE A LESSON TO YOU, WEEZIE -- DON'T **EVER** ASK ME TO DO ANYTHING NICE AGAIN!
AFTER IT WAS OVER, WE WATCHED STAR TREK IV ON CABLE WITHOUT SAYING A WORD. AFTER THAT I LEFT... I SAID I WAS GOING TO CALL HIM WHEN I GOT HOME BUT OBVIOUSLY I NEVER DID...
ONCE I GOT OUTSIDE I STARTED TO FEEL REALLY WEIRD... EVERYBODY WAS CHECKING ME OUT... I KEPT IMAGINING BECKY'S REACTION TO EVERYTHING. ESPECIALLY THE JEFFERSONS.

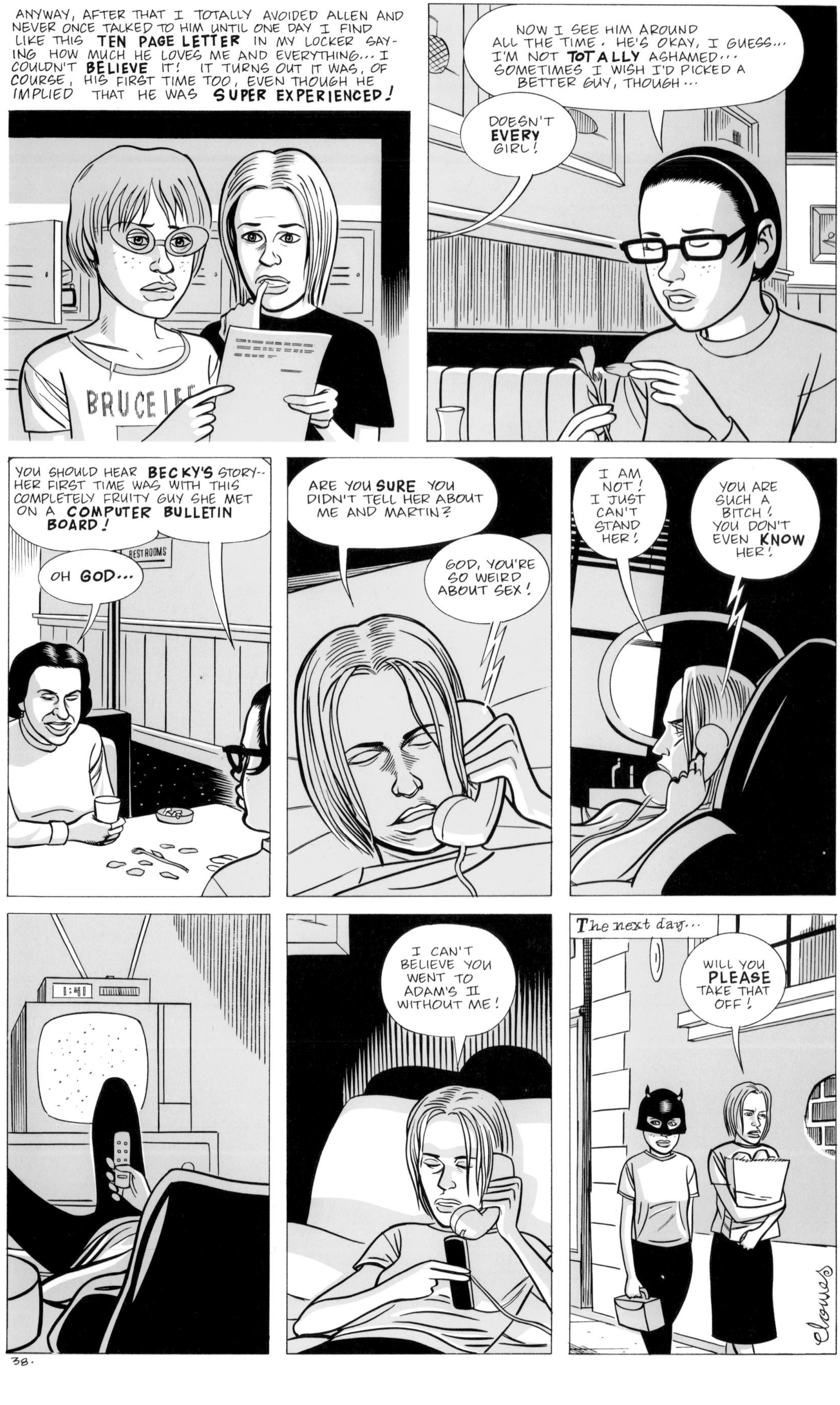

ANYWAY, AFTER THAT I TOTALLY AVOIDED ALLEN AND NEVER ONCE TALKED TO HIM UNTIL ONE DAY I FIND LIKE THIS TEN PAGE LETTER IN MY LOCKER SAYING HOW MUCH HE LOVES ME AND EVERYTHING... I COULDN'T BELIEVE IT! IT TURNS OUT IT WAS, OF COURSE, HIS FIRST TIME TOO, EVEN THOUGH HE IMPLIED THAT HE WAS SUPER EXPERIENCED!
BRUCE LEE
NOW I SEE HIM AROUND ALL THE TIME. HE'S OKAY, I GUESS... I'M NOT TOTALLY ASHAMED... SOMETIMES I WISH I'D PICKED A BETTER GUY, THOUGH...
DOESN'T EVERY GIRL!
YOU SHOULD HEAR BECKY'S STORY-- HER FIRST TIME WAS WITH THIS COMPLETELY FRUITY GUY SHE MET ON A COMPUTER BULLETIN BOARD!
RESTROOMS
OH GOD...
ARE YOU SURE YOU DIDN'T TELL HER ABOUT ME AND MARTIN?
GOD, YOU'RE SO WEIRD ABOUT SEX!
I AM NOT! I JUST CAN'T STAND HER!
YOU ARE SUCH A BITCH! YOU DON'T EVEN KNOW HER!
1:41
I CAN'T BELIEVE YOU WENT TO ADAM'S II WITHOUT ME!
The next day...
WILL YOU PLEASE TAKE THAT OFF!
clowes

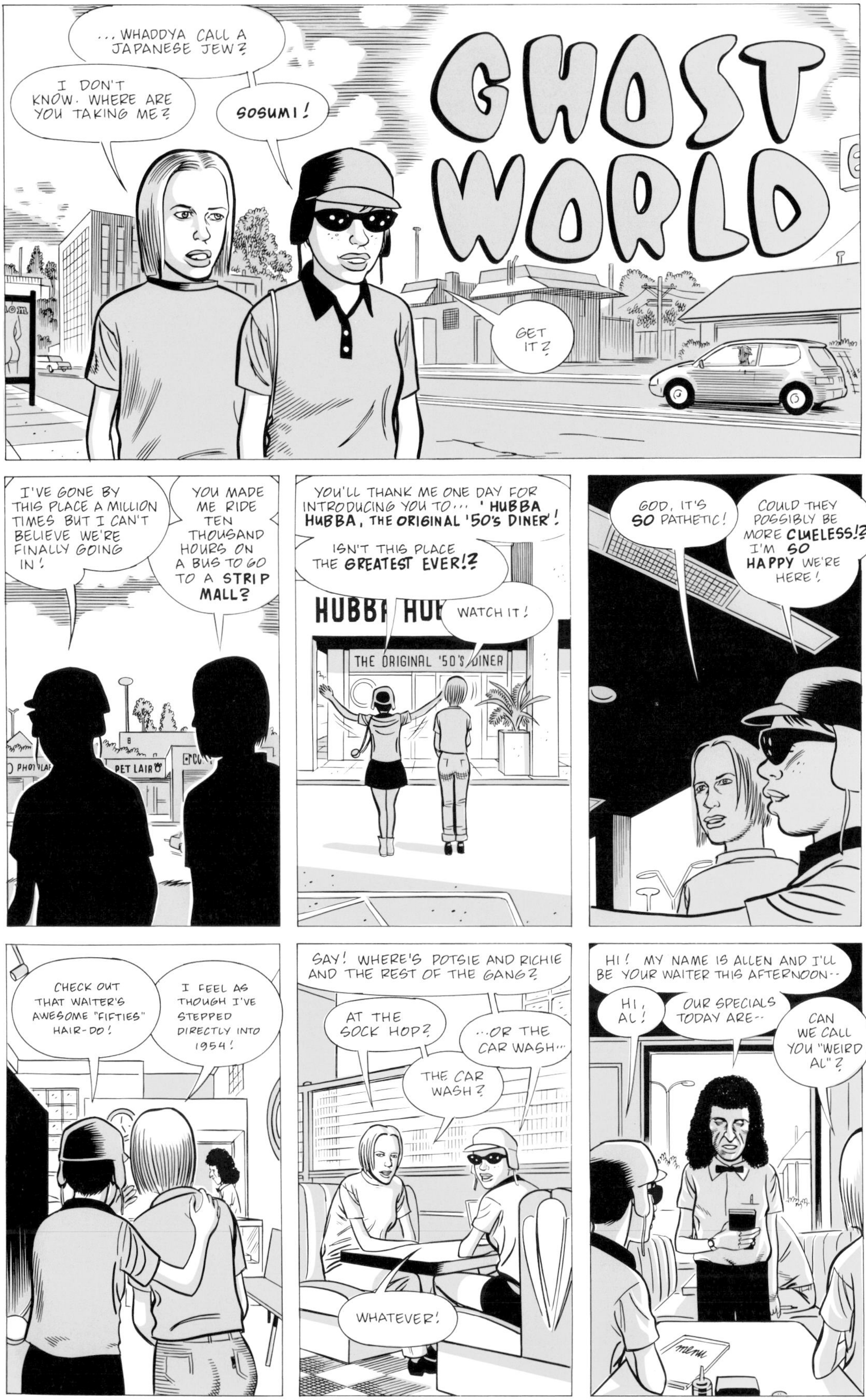
...WHADDYA CALL A JAPANESE JEW?
I DON'T KNOW. WHERE ARE YOU TAKING ME?
SOSUMI!
GHOST WORLD
GET IT?
I'VE GONE BY THIS PLACE A MILLION TIMES BUT I CAN'T BELIEVE WE'RE FINALLY GOING IN!
YOU MADE ME RIDE TEN THOUSAND HOURS ON A BUS TO GO TO A STRIP MALL?
PHOTO LAB
PET LAIR
YOU'LL THANK ME ONE DAY FOR INTRODUCING YOU TO... 'HUBBA HUBBA, THE ORIGINAL '50's DINER'!
ISN'T THIS PLACE THE GREATEST EVER!?
WATCH IT!
THE ORIGINAL '50's DINER
GOD, IT'S SO PATHETIC!
COULD THEY POSSIBLY BE MORE CLUELESS!? I'M SO HAPPY WE'RE HERE!
CHECK OUT THAT WAITER'S AWESOME "FIFTIES" HAIR-DO!
I FEEL AS THOUGH I'VE STEPPED DIRECTLY INTO 1954!
SAY! WHERE'S POTSIE AND RICHIE AND THE REST OF THE GANG?
AT THE SOCK HOP?
...OR THE CAR WASH...
THE CAR WASH?
WHATEVER!
HI! MY NAME IS ALLEN AND I'LL BE YOUR WAITER THIS AFTERNOON--
HI, AL!
OUR SPECIALS TODAY ARE--
CAN WE CALL YOU "WEIRD AL"?
menu

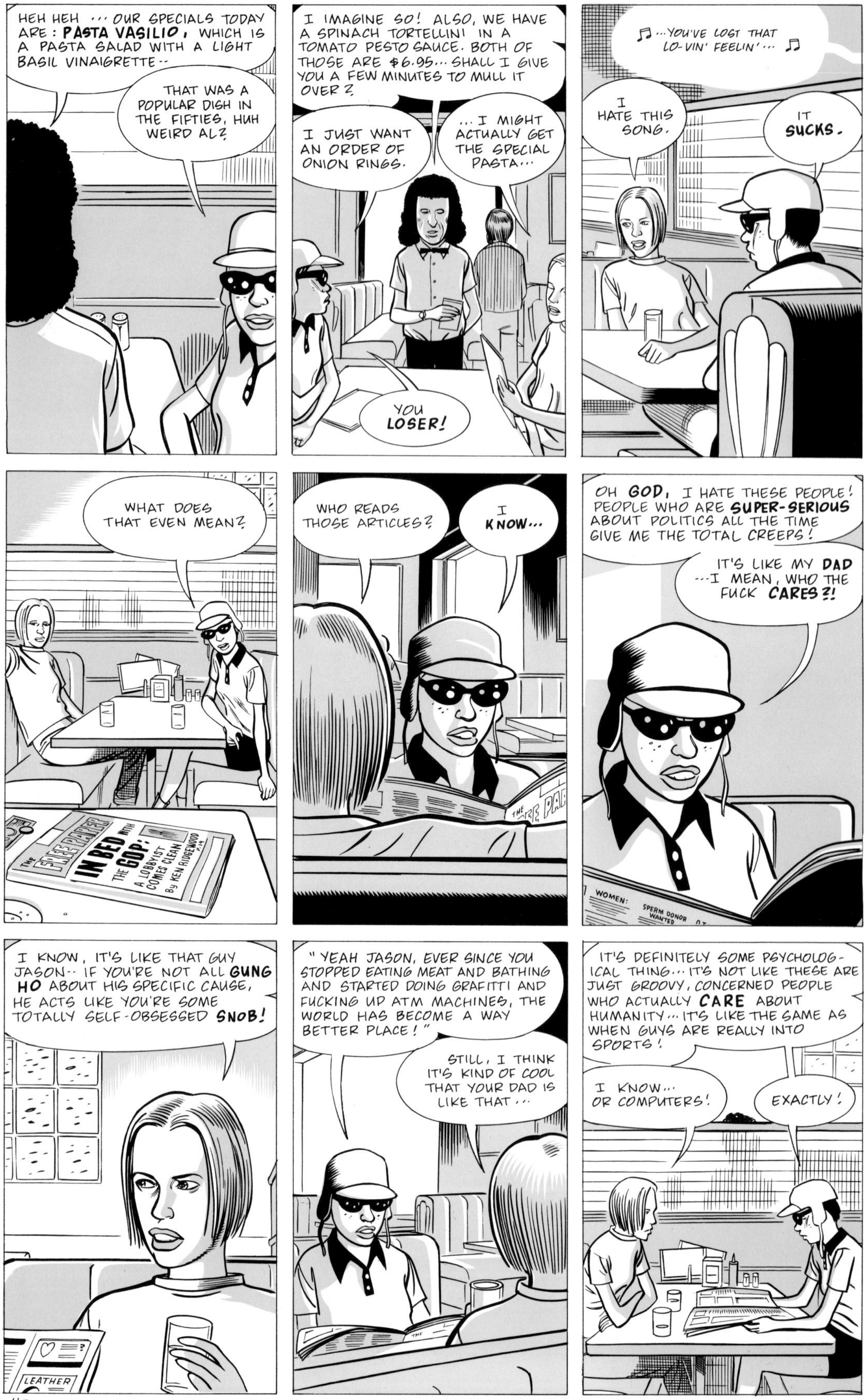
HEH HEH ... OUR SPECIALS TODAY ARE: PASTA VASILIO, WHICH IS A PASTA SALAD WITH A LIGHT BASIL VINAIGRETTE--
THAT WAS A POPULAR DISH IN THE FIFTIES, HUH WEIRD AL?
I IMAGINE SO! ALSO, WE HAVE A SPINACH TORTELLINI IN A TOMATO PESTO SAUCE. BOTH OF THOSE ARE $6.95... SHALL I GIVE YOU A FEW MINUTES TO MULL IT OVER?
I JUST WANT AN ORDER OF ONION RINGS.
...I MIGHT ACTUALLY GET THE SPECIAL PASTA...
YOU LOSER!
♫ ...YOU'VE LOST THAT LO-VIN' FEELIN'... ♫
I HATE THIS SONG.
IT SUCKS.
WHAT DOES THAT EVEN MEAN?
IN BED WITH THE GOP: A LOBBYIST COMES CLEAN
By KEN RIDGEWOOD
WHO READS THOSE ARTICLES?
I KNOW...
OH GOD, I HATE THESE PEOPLE! PEOPLE WHO ARE SUPER-SERIOUS ABOUT POLITICS ALL THE TIME GIVE ME THE TOTAL CREEPS!
IT'S LIKE MY DAD ...I MEAN, WHO THE FUCK CARES?!
WOMEN:
SPERM DONOR WANTED
I KNOW, IT'S LIKE THAT GUY JASON-- IF YOU'RE NOT ALL GUNG HO ABOUT HIS SPECIFIC CAUSE, HE ACTS LIKE YOU'RE SOME TOTALLY SELF-OBSESSED SNOB!
LEATHER
"YEAH JASON, EVER SINCE YOU STOPPED EATING MEAT AND BATHING AND STARTED DOING GRAFITTI AND FUCKING UP ATM MACHINES, THE WORLD HAS BECOME A WAY BETTER PLACE!"
STILL, I THINK IT'S KIND OF COOL THAT YOUR DAD IS LIKE THAT...
IT'S DEFINITELY SOME PSYCHOLOGICAL THING... IT'S NOT LIKE THESE ARE JUST GROOVY, CONCERNED PEOPLE WHO ACTUALLY CARE ABOUT HUMANITY... IT'S LIKE THE SAME AS WHEN GUYS ARE REALLY INTO SPORTS!
I KNOW... OR COMPUTERS!
EXACTLY!

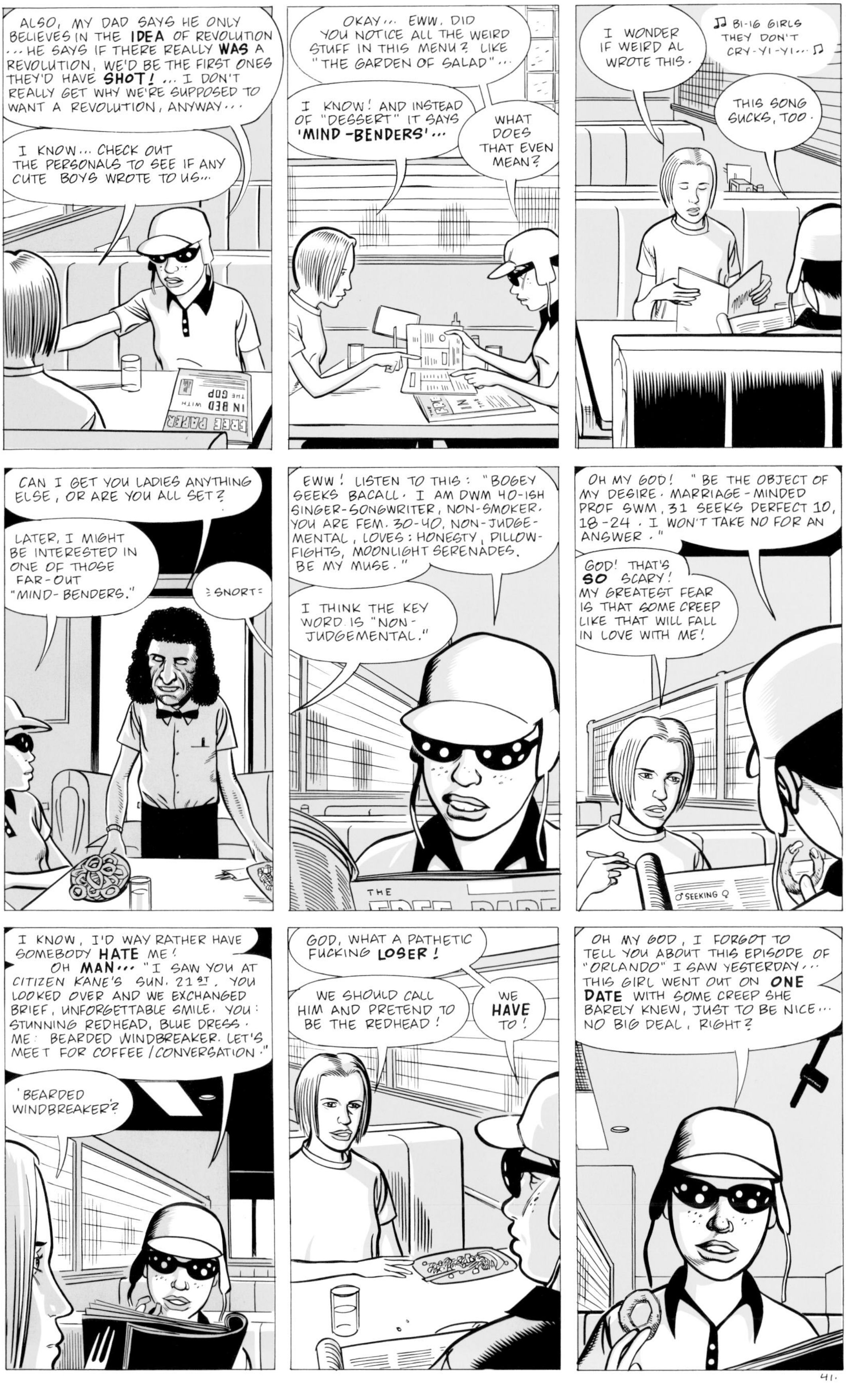

ALSO, MY DAD SAYS HE ONLY BELIEVES IN THE **IDEA** OF REVOLUTION ... HE SAYS IF THERE REALLY **WAS** A REVOLUTION, WE'D BE THE FIRST ONES THEY'D HAVE **SHOT!** ... I DON'T REALLY GET WHY WE'RE SUPPOSED TO WANT A REVOLUTION, ANYWAY...
I KNOW... CHECK OUT THE PERSONALS TO SEE IF ANY CUTE BOYS WROTE TO US...
FREE PAPER
IN BED WITH THE GOP
OKAY... EWW. DID YOU NOTICE ALL THE WEIRD STUFF IN THIS MENU? LIKE "THE GARDEN OF SALAD"...
I KNOW! AND INSTEAD OF "DESSERT" IT SAYS **'MIND-BENDERS'...**
WHAT DOES THAT EVEN MEAN?
I WONDER IF WEIRD AL WROTE THIS.
♫ BI-16 GIRLS THEY DON'T CRY-YI-YI... ♫
THIS SONG SUCKS, TOO.
CAN I GET YOU LADIES ANYTHING ELSE, OR ARE YOU ALL SET?
LATER, I MIGHT BE INTERESTED IN ONE OF THOSE FAR-OUT "MIND-BENDERS."
SNORT
EWW! LISTEN TO THIS: "BOGEY SEEKS BACALL. I AM DWM 40-ISH SINGER-SONGWRITER, NON-SMOKER. YOU ARE FEM. 30-40, NON-JUDGEMENTAL, LOVES: HONESTY, PILLOW-FIGHTS, MOONLIGHT SERENADES. BE MY MUSE."
I THINK THE KEY WORD IS "NON-JUDGEMENTAL."
THE
OH MY GOD! "BE THE OBJECT OF MY DESIRE. MARRIAGE-MINDED PROF SWM, 31 SEEKS PERFECT 10, 18-24. I WON'T TAKE NO FOR AN ANSWER."
GOD! THAT'S **SO** SCARY! MY GREATEST FEAR IS THAT SOME CREEP LIKE THAT WILL FALL IN LOVE WITH ME!
♂ SEEKING ♀
I KNOW, I'D WAY RATHER HAVE SOMEBODY **HATE** ME! OH **MAN...** "I SAW YOU AT CITIZEN KANE'S SUN. 21ST. YOU LOOKED OVER AND WE EXCHANGED BRIEF, UNFORGETTABLE SMILE. YOU: STUNNING REDHEAD, BLUE DRESS. ME: BEARDED WINDBREAKER. LET'S MEET FOR COFFEE/CONVERSATION."
'BEARDED WINDBREAKER'?
GOD, WHAT A PATHETIC FUCKING **LOSER!**
WE SHOULD CALL HIM AND PRETEND TO BE THE REDHEAD!
WE **HAVE** TO!
OH MY GOD, I FORGOT TO TELL YOU ABOUT THIS EPISODE OF "ORLANDO" I SAW YESTERDAY... THIS GIRL WENT OUT ON **ONE DATE** WITH SOME CREEP SHE BARELY KNEW, JUST TO BE NICE... NO BIG DEAL, RIGHT?

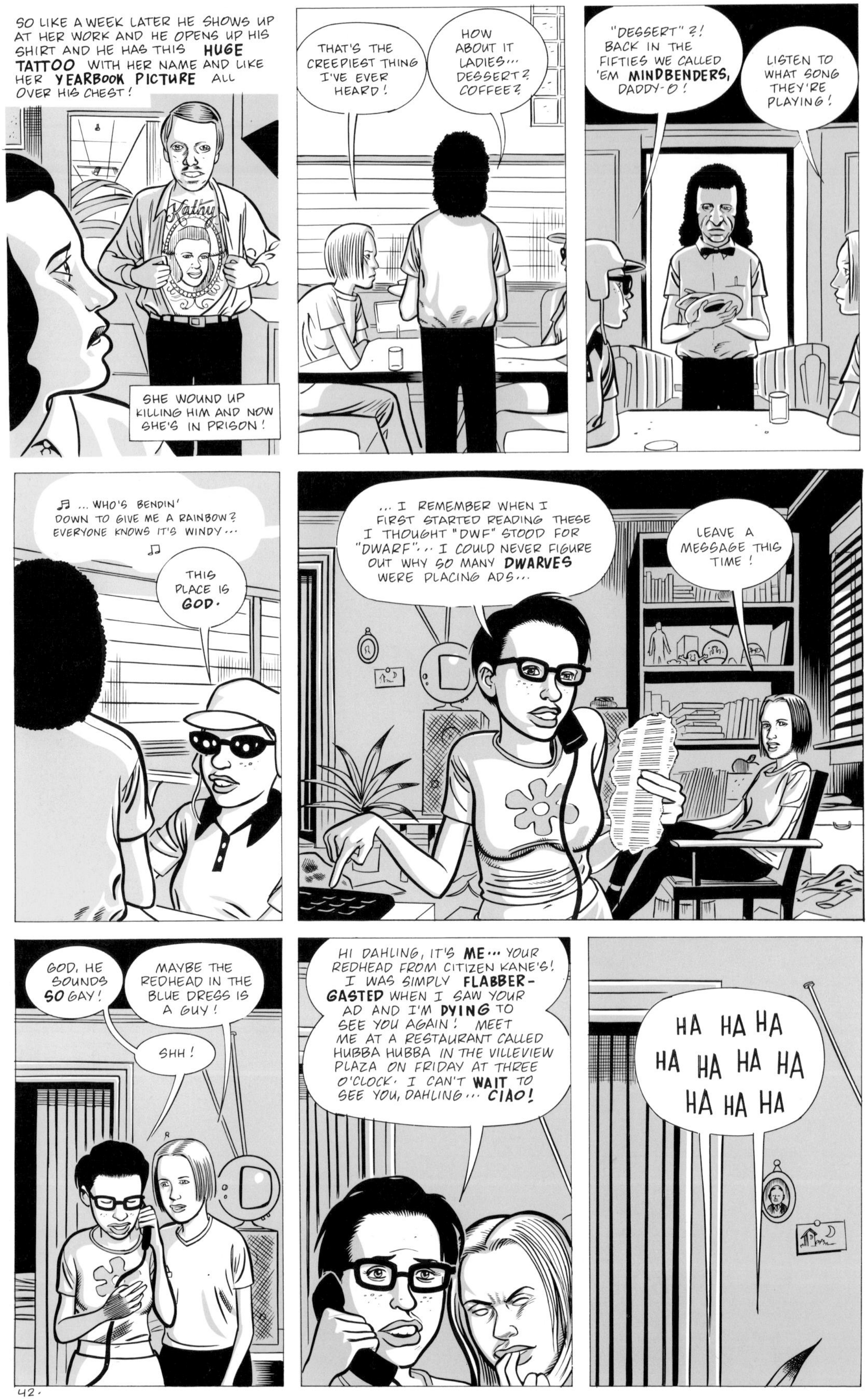
SO LIKE A WEEK LATER HE SHOWS UP AT HER WORK AND HE OPENS UP HIS SHIRT AND HE HAS THIS HUGE TATTOO WITH HER NAME AND LIKE HER YEARBOOK PICTURE ALL OVER HIS CHEST!
Kathy
SHE WOUND UP KILLING HIM AND NOW SHE'S IN PRISON!
THAT'S THE CREEPIEST THING I'VE EVER HEARD!
HOW ABOUT IT LADIES... DESSERT? COFFEE?
"DESSERT"?! BACK IN THE FIFTIES WE CALLED 'EM MINDBENDERS, DADDY-O!
LISTEN TO WHAT SONG THEY'RE PLAYING!
♫ ... WHO'S BENDIN' DOWN TO GIVE ME A RAINBOW? EVERYONE KNOWS IT'S WINDY... ♫
THIS PLACE IS GOD.
... I REMEMBER WHEN I FIRST STARTED READING THESE I THOUGHT "DWF" STOOD FOR "DWARF"... I COULD NEVER FIGURE OUT WHY SO MANY DWARVES WERE PLACING ADS...
LEAVE A MESSAGE THIS TIME!
GOD, HE SOUNDS SO GAY!
MAYBE THE REDHEAD IN THE BLUE DRESS IS A GUY!
SHH!
HI DAHLING, IT'S ME... YOUR REDHEAD FROM CITIZEN KANE'S! I WAS SIMPLY FLABBERGASTED WHEN I SAW YOUR AD AND I'M DYING TO SEE YOU AGAIN! MEET ME AT A RESTAURANT CALLED HUBBA HUBBA IN THE VILLEVIEW PLAZA ON FRIDAY AT THREE O'CLOCK. I CAN'T WAIT TO SEE YOU, DAHLING... CIAO!
HA HA HA HA HA HA HA HA HA HA

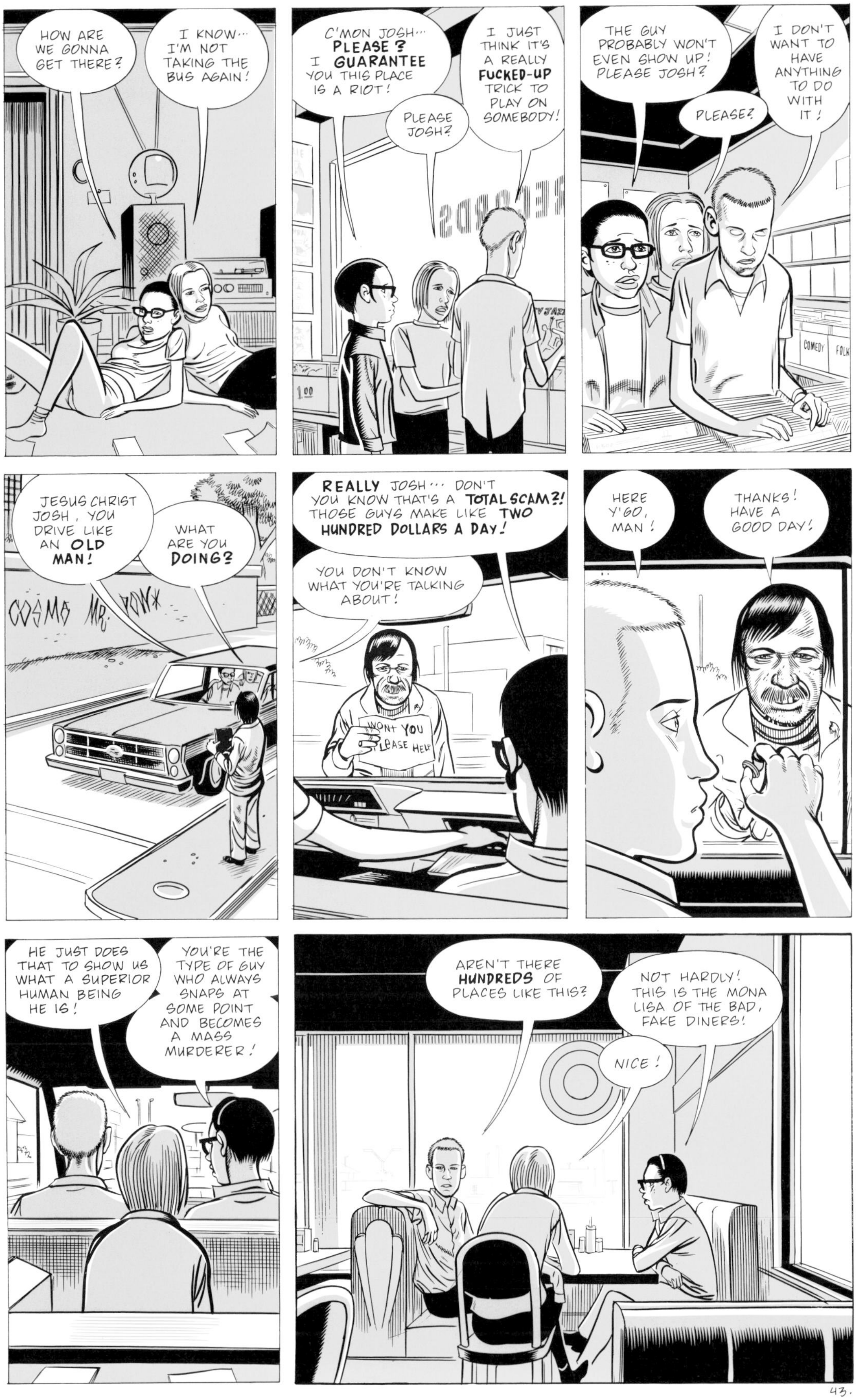
HOW ARE WE GONNA GET THERE?
I KNOW... I'M NOT TAKING THE BUS AGAIN!
C'MON JOSH... **PLEASE?** I **GUARANTEE** YOU THIS PLACE IS A RIOT!
PLEASE JOSH?
I JUST THINK IT'S A REALLY **FUCKED-UP** TRICK TO PLAY ON SOMEBODY!
THE GUY PROBABLY WON'T EVEN SHOW UP! PLEASE JOSH?
PLEASE?
I DON'T WANT TO HAVE ANYTHING TO DO WITH IT!
COMEDY
FOLK
JESUS CHRIST JOSH, YOU DRIVE LIKE AN **OLD MAN!**
WHAT ARE YOU **DOING?**
REALLY JOSH... DON'T YOU KNOW THAT'S A **TOTAL SCAM?!** THOSE GUYS MAKE LIKE **TWO HUNDRED DOLLARS A DAY!**
YOU DON'T KNOW WHAT YOU'RE TALKING ABOUT!
HERE Y'GO, MAN!
THANKS! HAVE A GOOD DAY!
HE JUST DOES THAT TO SHOW US WHAT A SUPERIOR HUMAN BEING HE IS!
YOU'RE THE TYPE OF GUY WHO ALWAYS SNAPS AT SOME POINT AND BECOMES A MASS MURDERER!
AREN'T THERE **HUNDREDS** OF PLACES LIKE THIS?
NOT HARDLY! THIS IS THE MONA LISA OF THE BAD, FAKE DINERS!
NICE!

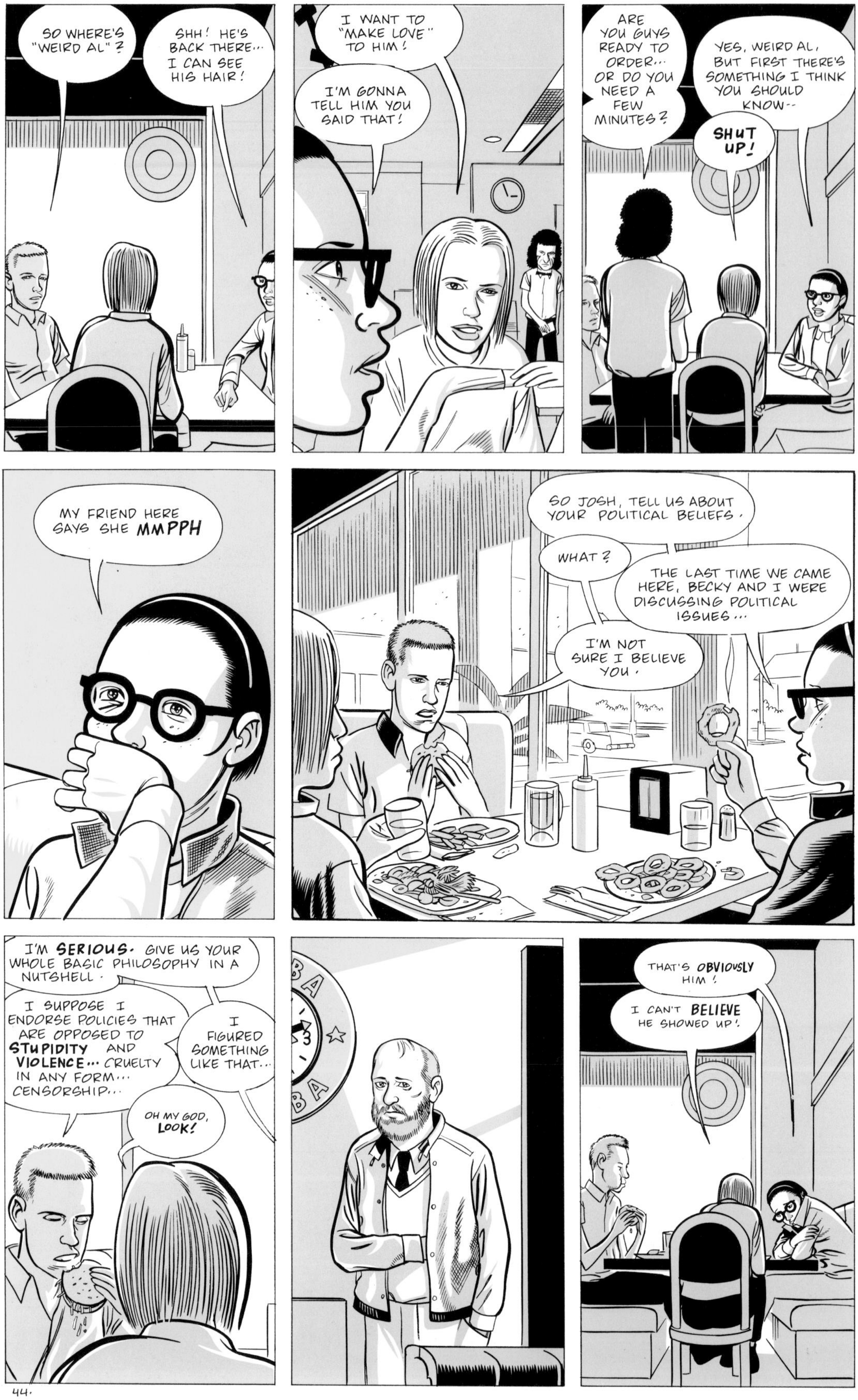
SO WHERE'S "WEIRD AL"?
SHH! HE'S BACK THERE... I CAN SEE HIS HAIR!
I WANT TO "MAKE LOVE" TO HIM!
I'M GONNA TELL HIM YOU SAID THAT!
ARE YOU GUYS READY TO ORDER... OR DO YOU NEED A FEW MINUTES?
YES, WEIRD AL, BUT FIRST THERE'S SOMETHING I THINK YOU SHOULD KNOW--
SHUT UP!
MY FRIEND HERE SAYS SHE MMPPH
SO JOSH, TELL US ABOUT YOUR POLITICAL BELIEFS.
WHAT?
THE LAST TIME WE CAME HERE, BECKY AND I WERE DISCUSSING POLITICAL ISSUES...
I'M NOT SURE I BELIEVE YOU.
I'M SERIOUS. GIVE US YOUR WHOLE BASIC PHILOSOPHY IN A NUTSHELL.
I SUPPOSE I ENDORSE POLICIES THAT ARE OPPOSED TO STUPIDITY AND VIOLENCE... CRUELTY IN ANY FORM... CENSORSHIP...
I FIGURED SOMETHING LIKE THAT...
OH MY GOD, LOOK!
THAT'S OBVIOUSLY HIM!
I CAN'T BELIEVE HE SHOWED UP!

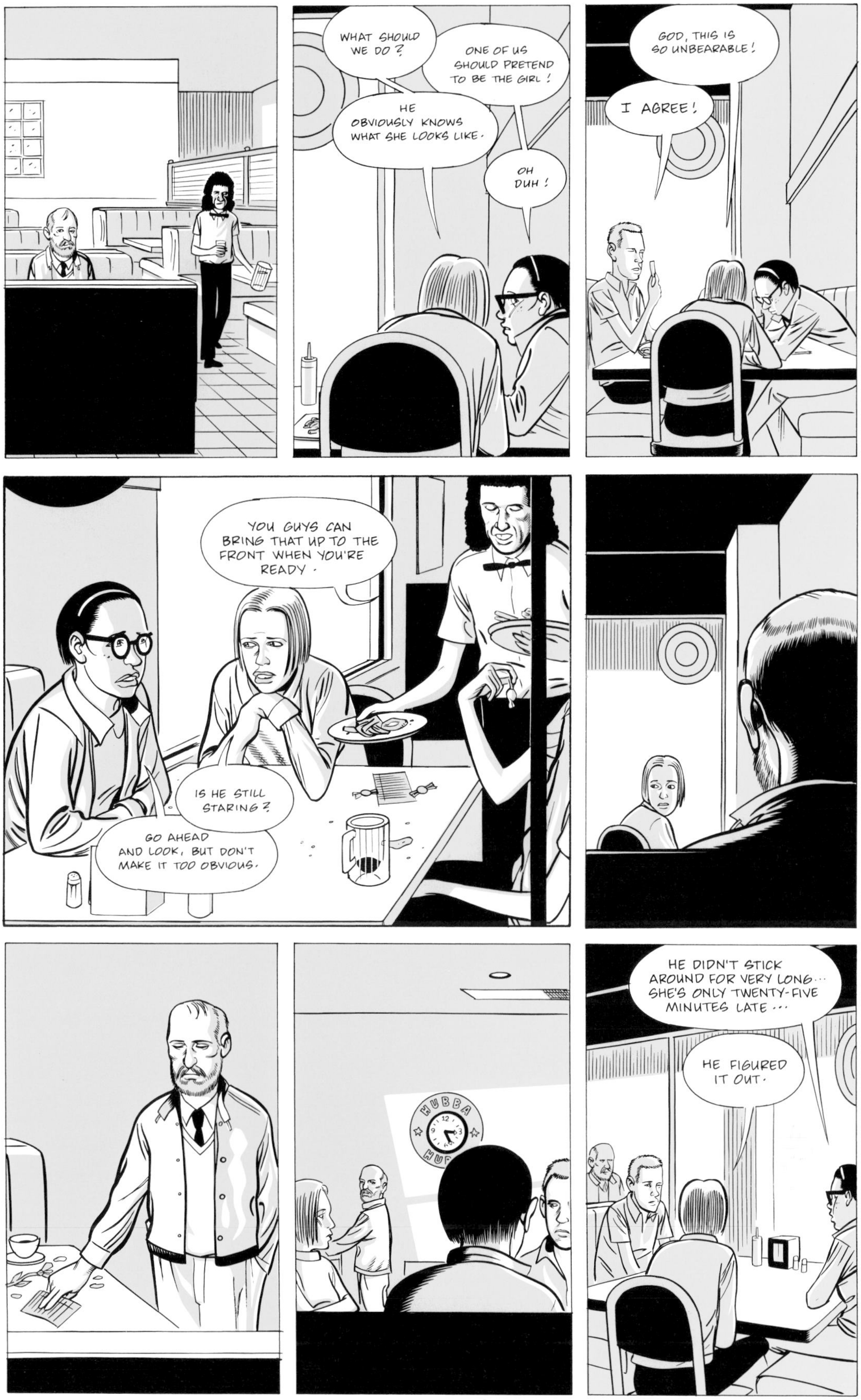
WHAT SHOULD WE DO?
ONE OF US SHOULD PRETEND TO BE THE GIRL!
HE OBVIOUSLY KNOWS WHAT SHE LOOKS LIKE.
OH DUH!
GOD, THIS IS SO UNBEARABLE!
I AGREE!
YOU GUYS CAN BRING THAT UP TO THE FRONT WHEN YOU'RE READY.
IS HE STILL STARING?
GO AHEAD AND LOOK, BUT DON'T MAKE IT TOO OBVIOUS.
HUBBA HUB
HE DIDN'T STICK AROUND FOR VERY LONG... SHE'S ONLY TWENTY-FIVE MINUTES LATE...
HE FIGURED IT OUT.

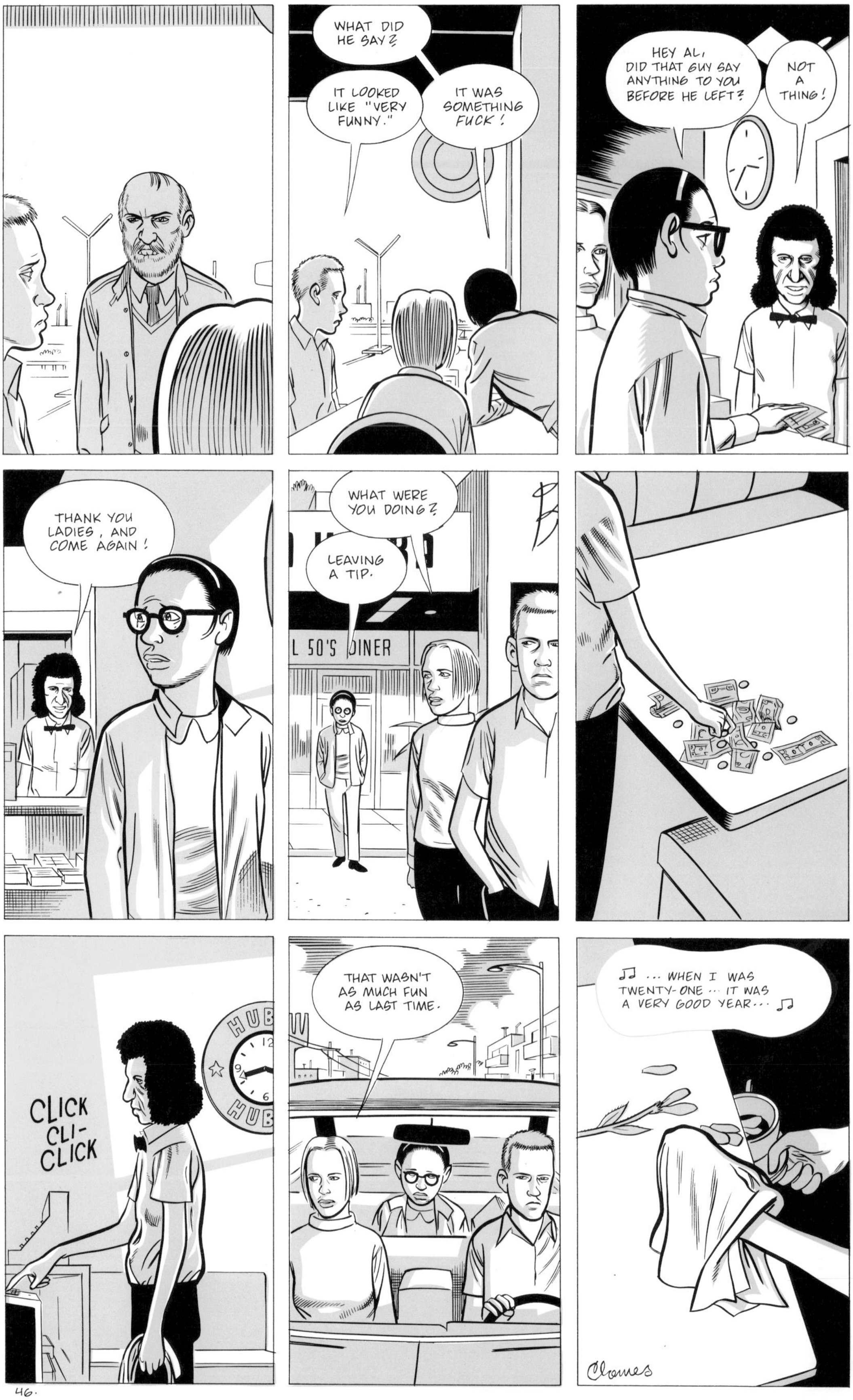
WHAT DID HE SAY?
IT LOOKED LIKE "VERY FUNNY."
IT WAS SOMETHING FUCK!
HEY AL, DID THAT GUY SAY ANYTHING TO YOU BEFORE HE LEFT?
NOT A THING!
THANK YOU LADIES, AND COME AGAIN!
WHAT WERE YOU DOING?
LEAVING A TIP.
L 50'S DINER
CLICK CLI-CLICK
HUB
HUB
THAT WASN'T AS MUCH FUN AS LAST TIME.
♫ ... WHEN I WAS TWENTY-ONE ... IT WAS A VERY GOOD YEAR ... ♫
Clowes

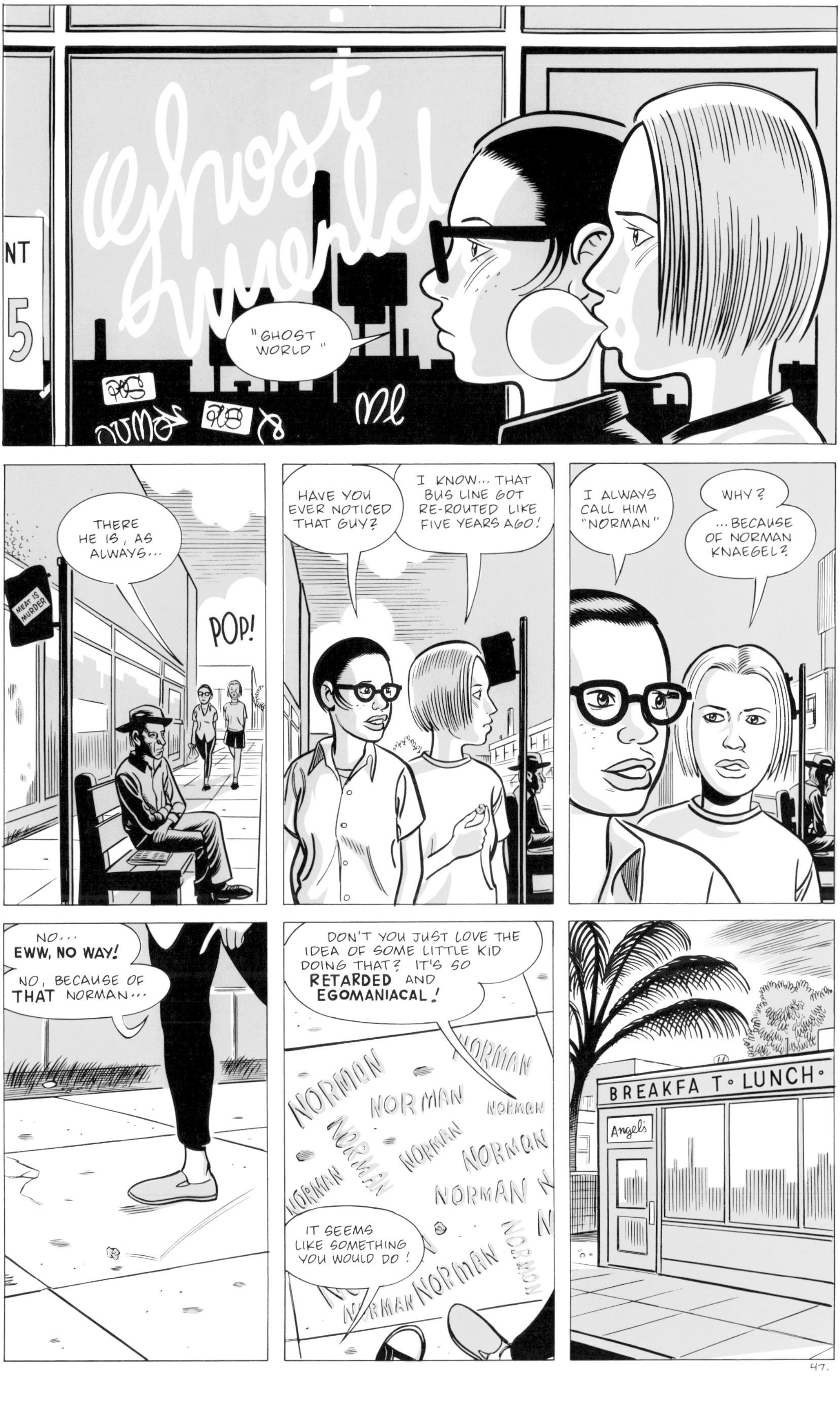
Ghost World
NT
5
"GHOST WORLD"
THERE HE IS, AS ALWAYS...
MEAT IS MURDER
POP!
HAVE YOU EVER NOTICED THAT GUY?
I KNOW... THAT BUS LINE GOT RE-ROUTED LIKE FIVE YEARS AGO!
I ALWAYS CALL HIM "NORMAN"
WHY?
...BECAUSE OF NORMAN KNAEGEL?
NO... **EWW, NO WAY!**
NO, BECAUSE OF **THAT** NORMAN...
DON'T YOU JUST LOVE THE IDEA OF SOME LITTLE KID DOING THAT? IT'S SO **RETARDED** AND **EGOMANIACAL**!
NORMAN NORMAN NORMAN NORMAN NORMAN NORMAN NORMAN NORMAN NORMAN NORMAN NORMAN NORMAN NORMAN
IT SEEMS LIKE SOMETHING YOU WOULD DO!
BREAKFA T · LUNCH ·
Angels

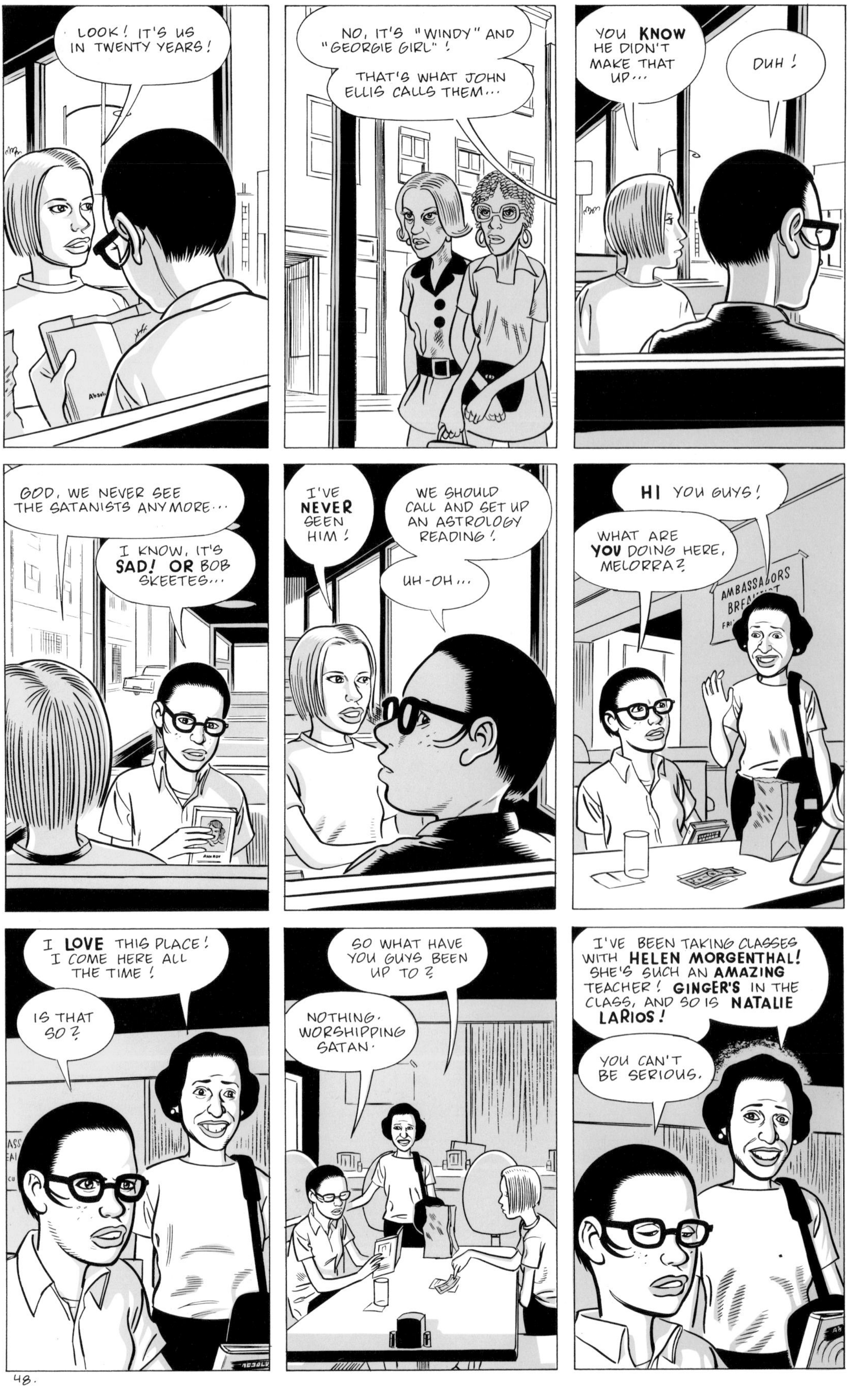
LOOK! IT'S US IN TWENTY YEARS!
NO, IT'S "WINDY" AND "GEORGIE GIRL"!
THAT'S WHAT JOHN ELLIS CALLS THEM...
YOU KNOW HE DIDN'T MAKE THAT UP...
DUH!
GOD, WE NEVER SEE THE SATANISTS ANYMORE...
I KNOW, IT'S SAD! OR BOB SKEETES...
I'VE NEVER SEEN HIM!
WE SHOULD CALL AND SET UP AN ASTROLOGY READING!
UH-OH...
HI YOU GUYS!
WHAT ARE YOU DOING HERE, MELORRA?
AMBASSADORS
I LOVE THIS PLACE! I COME HERE ALL THE TIME!
IS THAT SO?
SO WHAT HAVE YOU GUYS BEEN UP TO?
NOTHING. WORSHIPPING SATAN.
I'VE BEEN TAKING CLASSES WITH HELEN MORGENTHAL! SHE'S SUCH AN AMAZING TEACHER! GINGER'S IN THE CLASS, AND SO IS NATALIE LARIOS!
YOU CAN'T BE SERIOUS.

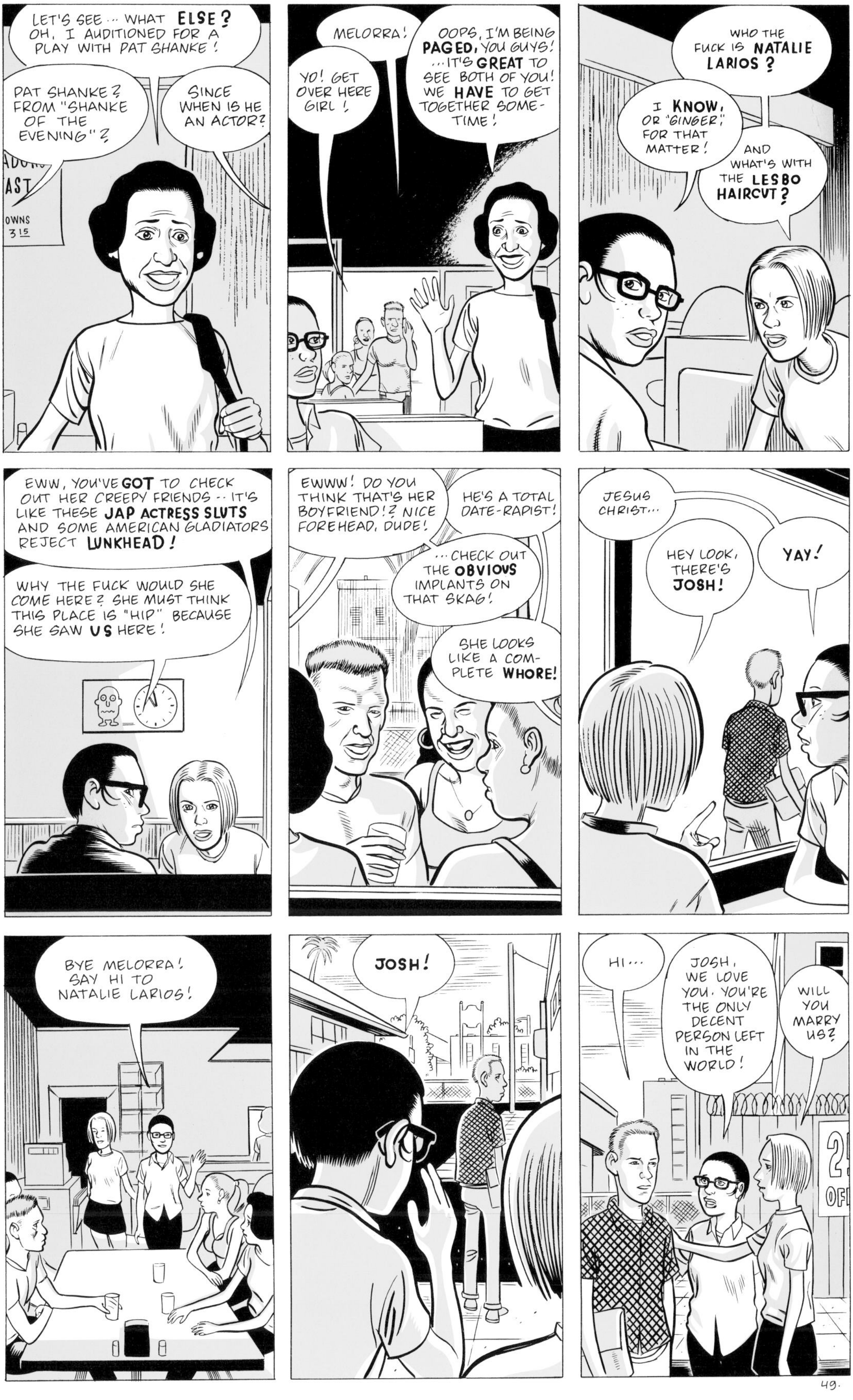
LET'S SEE... WHAT ELSE? OH, I AUDITIONED FOR A PLAY WITH PAT SHANKE!
PAT SHANKE? FROM "SHANKE OF THE EVENING"?
SINCE WHEN IS HE AN ACTOR?
MELORRA!
YO! GET OVER HERE GIRL!
OOPS, I'M BEING PAGED, YOU GUYS! ...IT'S GREAT TO SEE BOTH OF YOU! WE HAVE TO GET TOGETHER SOME-TIME!
WHO THE FUCK IS NATALIE LARIOS?
I KNOW, OR "GINGER," FOR THAT MATTER!
AND WHAT'S WITH THE LESBO HAIRCUT?
EWW, YOU'VE GOT TO CHECK OUT HER CREEPY FRIENDS -- IT'S LIKE THESE JAP ACTRESS SLUTS AND SOME AMERICAN GLADIATORS REJECT LUNKHEAD!
WHY THE FUCK WOULD SHE COME HERE? SHE MUST THINK THIS PLACE IS "HIP" BECAUSE SHE SAW US HERE!
EWWW! DO YOU THINK THAT'S HER BOYFRIEND!? NICE FOREHEAD, DUDE!
HE'S A TOTAL DATE-RAPIST!
...CHECK OUT THE OBVIOUS IMPLANTS ON THAT SKAG!
SHE LOOKS LIKE A COM-PLETE WHORE!
JESUS CHRIST...
HEY LOOK, THERE'S JOSH!
YAY!
BYE MELORRA! SAY HI TO NATALIE LARIOS!
JOSH!
HI...
JOSH, WE LOVE YOU. YOU'RE THE ONLY DECENT PERSON LEFT IN THE WORLD!
WILL YOU MARRY US?

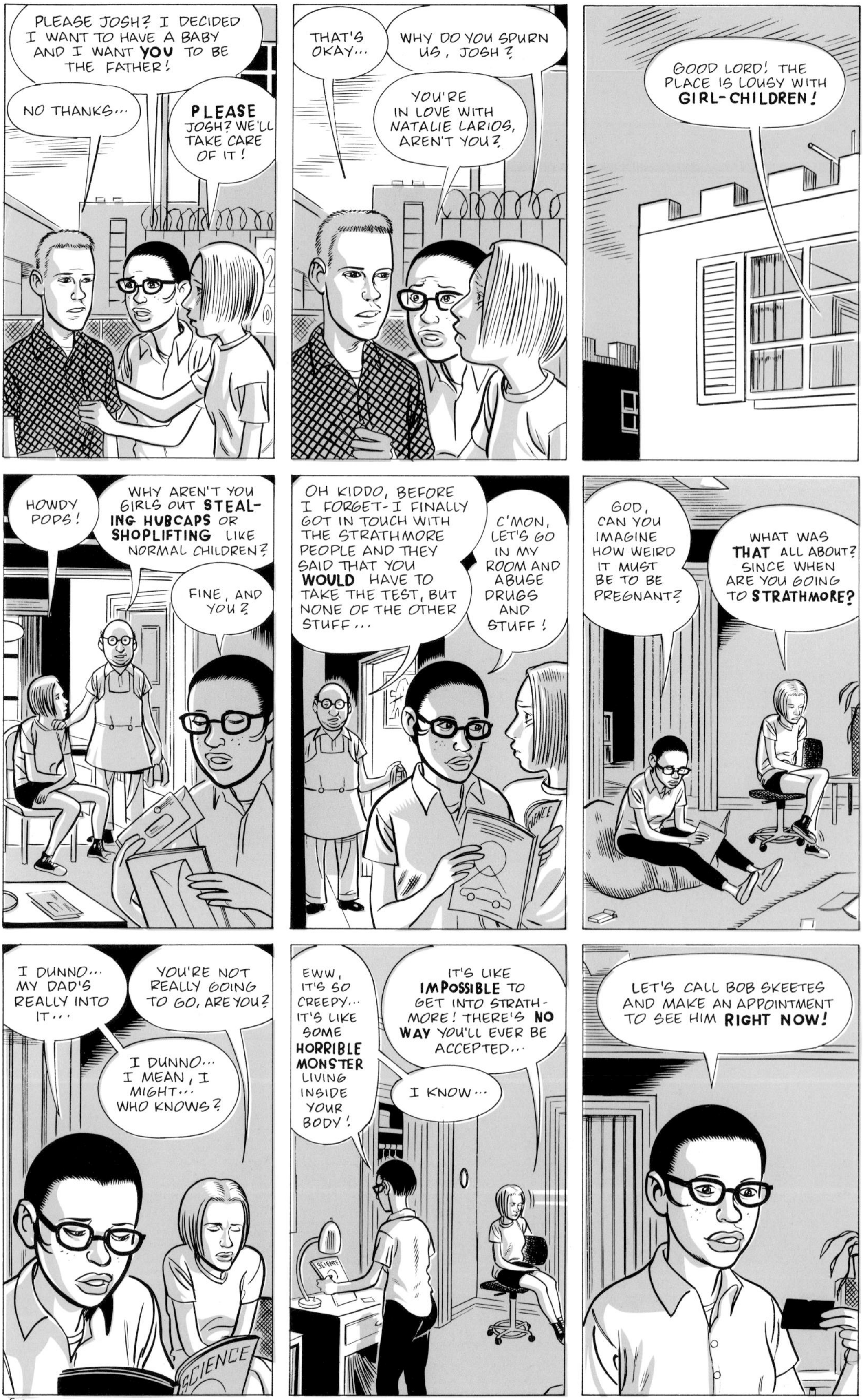
PLEASE JOSH? I DECIDED I WANT TO HAVE A BABY AND I WANT **YOU** TO BE THE FATHER!
NO THANKS...
PLEASE JOSH? WE'LL TAKE CARE OF IT!
THAT'S OKAY...
WHY DO YOU SPURN US, JOSH?
YOU'RE IN LOVE WITH NATALIE LARIOS, AREN'T YOU?
GOOD LORD! THE PLACE IS LOUSY WITH **GIRL-CHILDREN!**
HOWDY POPS!
WHY AREN'T YOU GIRLS OUT **STEALING HUBCAPS** OR **SHOPLIFTING** LIKE NORMAL CHILDREN?
FINE, AND YOU?
OH KIDDO, BEFORE I FORGET- I FINALLY GOT IN TOUCH WITH THE STRATHMORE PEOPLE AND THEY SAID THAT YOU **WOULD** HAVE TO TAKE THE TEST, BUT NONE OF THE OTHER STUFF...
C'MON, LET'S GO IN MY ROOM AND ABUSE DRUGS AND STUFF!
GOD, CAN YOU IMAGINE HOW WEIRD IT MUST BE TO BE PREGNANT?
WHAT WAS **THAT** ALL ABOUT? SINCE WHEN ARE YOU GOING TO **STRATHMORE?**
I DUNNO... MY DAD'S REALLY INTO IT...
YOU'RE NOT REALLY GOING TO GO, ARE YOU?
I DUNNO... I MEAN, I MIGHT... WHO KNOWS?
SCIENCE
EWW, IT'S SO CREEPY... IT'S LIKE SOME **HORRIBLE MONSTER** LIVING INSIDE YOUR BODY!
IT'S LIKE **IMPOSSIBLE** TO GET INTO STRATHMORE! THERE'S **NO WAY** YOU'LL EVER BE ACCEPTED...
I KNOW...
LET'S CALL BOB SKEETES AND MAKE AN APPOINTMENT TO SEE HIM **RIGHT NOW!**

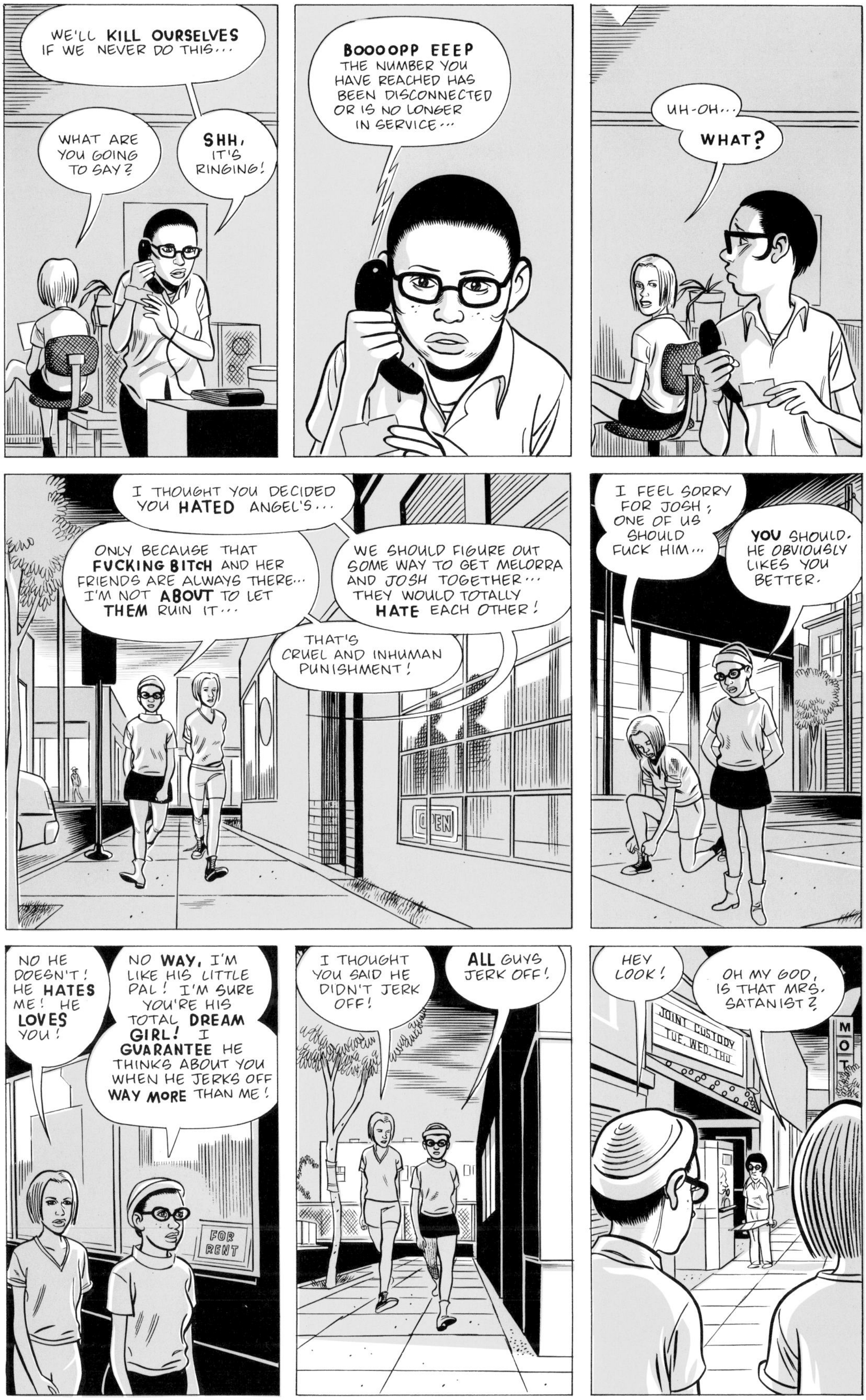
WE'LL KILL OURSELVES IF WE NEVER DO THIS...
WHAT ARE YOU GOING TO SAY?
SHH, IT'S RINGING!
BOOOOPP EEEP THE NUMBER YOU HAVE REACHED HAS BEEN DISCONNECTED OR IS NO LONGER IN SERVICE...
UH-OH...
WHAT?
I THOUGHT YOU DECIDED YOU HATED ANGEL'S...
ONLY BECAUSE THAT FUCKING BITCH AND HER FRIENDS ARE ALWAYS THERE... I'M NOT ABOUT TO LET THEM RUIN IT...
WE SHOULD FIGURE OUT SOME WAY TO GET MELORRA AND JOSH TOGETHER... THEY WOULD TOTALLY HATE EACH OTHER!
THAT'S CRUEL AND INHUMAN PUNISHMENT!
OPEN
I FEEL SORRY FOR JOSH; ONE OF US SHOULD FUCK HIM...
YOU SHOULD. HE OBVIOUSLY LIKES YOU BETTER.
NO HE DOESN'T! HE HATES ME! HE LOVES YOU!
NO WAY, I'M LIKE HIS LITTLE PAL! I'M SURE YOU'RE HIS TOTAL DREAM GIRL! I GUARANTEE HE THINKS ABOUT YOU WHEN HE JERKS OFF WAY MORE THAN ME!
FOR RENT
I THOUGHT YOU SAID HE DIDN'T JERK OFF!
ALL GUYS JERK OFF!
HEY LOOK!
OH MY GOD, IS THAT MRS. SATANIST?
JOINT CUSTODY
TUE. WED. THU
MOT

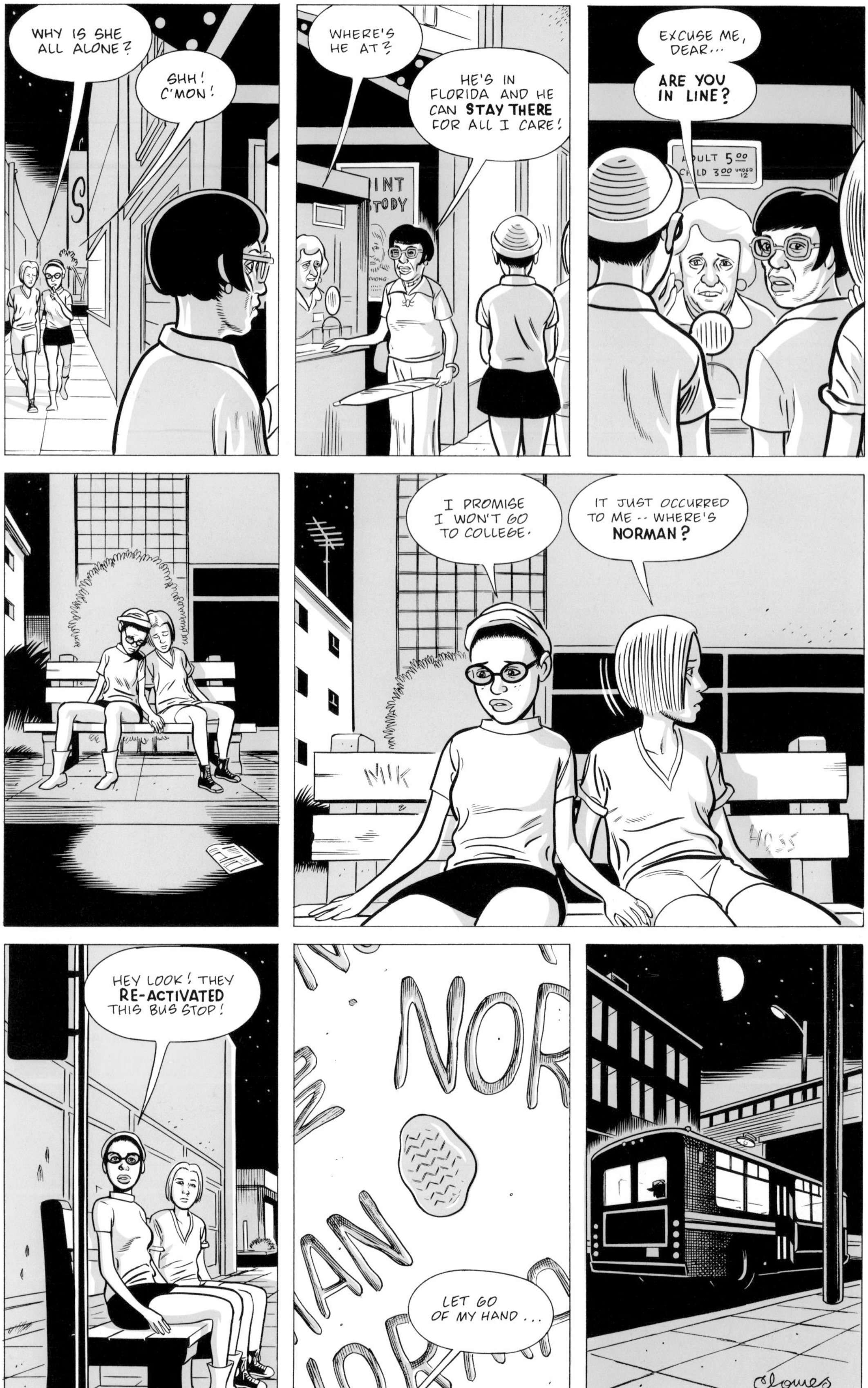
WHY IS SHE ALL ALONE?
SHH! C'MON!
WHERE'S HE AT?
HE'S IN FLORIDA AND HE CAN **STAY THERE** FOR ALL I CARE!
EXCUSE ME, DEAR...
ARE YOU IN LINE?
ADULT 5.00
CHILD 3.00 UNDER 12
I PROMISE I WON'T GO TO COLLEGE.
IT JUST OCCURRED TO ME -- WHERE'S **NORMAN?**
MIK
HOSS
HEY LOOK! THEY **RE-ACTIVATED** THIS BUS STOP!
NOR
LET GO OF MY HAND...
Clowes

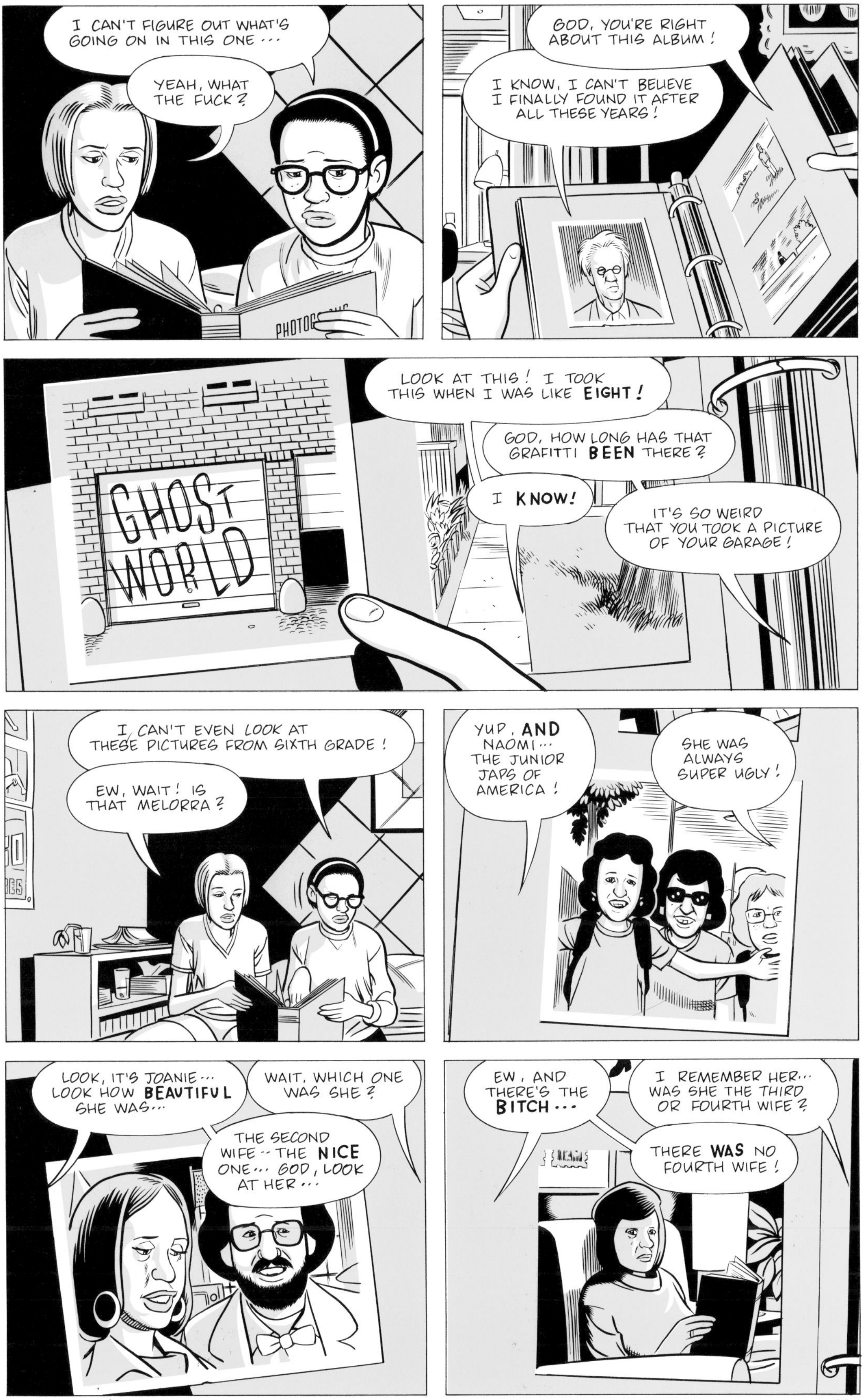
I CAN'T FIGURE OUT WHAT'S GOING ON IN THIS ONE ...
YEAH, WHAT THE FUCK?
GOD, YOU'RE RIGHT ABOUT THIS ALBUM!
I KNOW, I CAN'T BELIEVE I FINALLY FOUND IT AFTER ALL THESE YEARS!
LOOK AT THIS! I TOOK THIS WHEN I WAS LIKE EIGHT!
GOD, HOW LONG HAS THAT GRAFITTI BEEN THERE?
I KNOW!
IT'S SO WEIRD THAT YOU TOOK A PICTURE OF YOUR GARAGE!
GHOST WORLD
I CAN'T EVEN LOOK AT THESE PICTURES FROM SIXTH GRADE!
EW, WAIT! IS THAT MELORRA?
YUP, AND NAOMI... THE JUNIOR JAPS OF AMERICA!
SHE WAS ALWAYS SUPER UGLY!
LOOK, IT'S JOANIE... LOOK HOW BEAUTIFUL SHE WAS...
WAIT, WHICH ONE WAS SHE?
THE SECOND WIFE -- THE NICE ONE... GOD, LOOK AT HER...
EW, AND THERE'S THE BITCH...
I REMEMBER HER... WAS SHE THE THIRD OR FOURTH WIFE?
THERE WAS NO FOURTH WIFE!

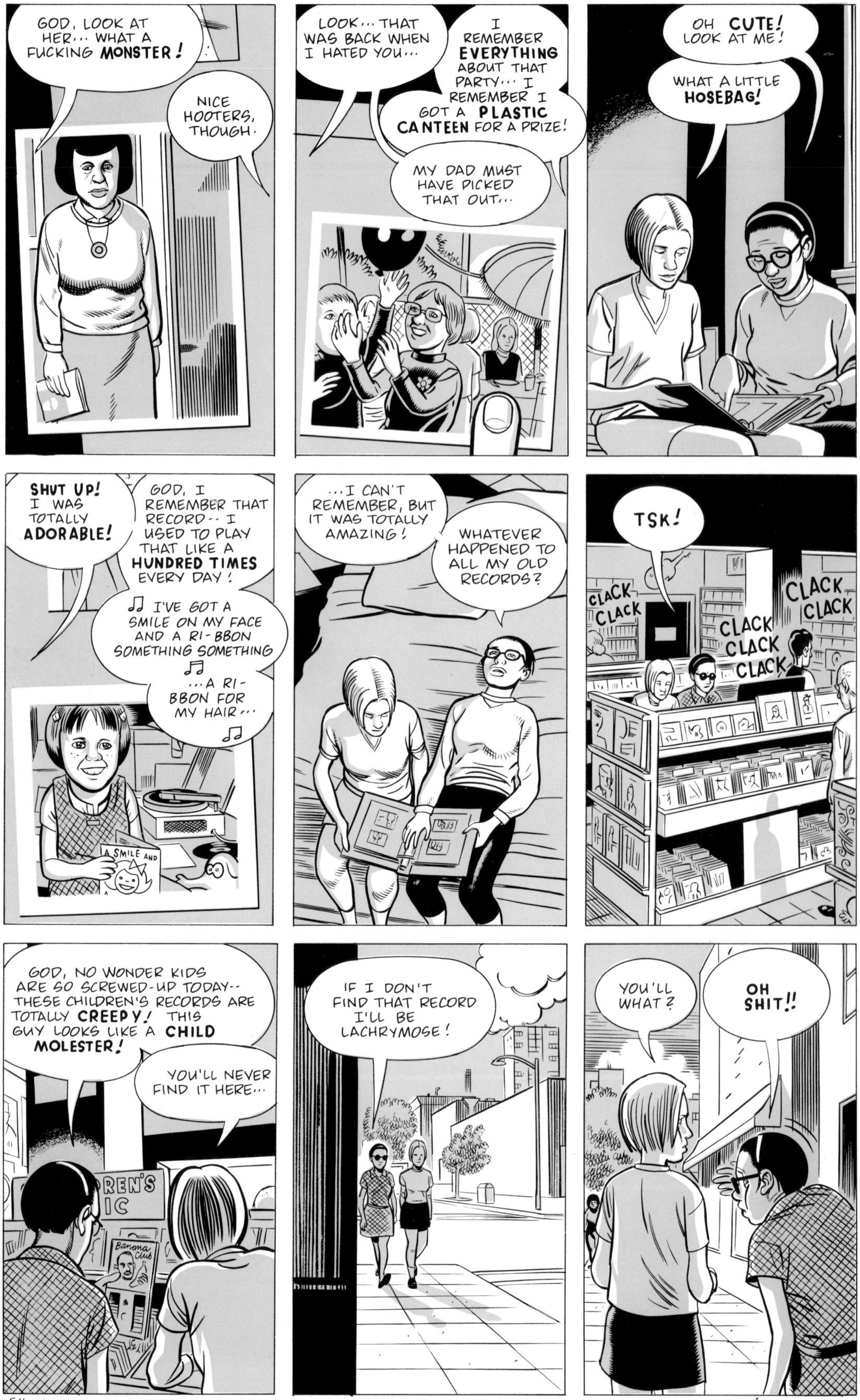
GOD, LOOK AT HER... WHAT A FUCKING **MONSTER**!
NICE HOOTERS, THOUGH.
LOOK... THAT WAS BACK WHEN I HATED YOU...
I REMEMBER **EVERYTHING** ABOUT THAT PARTY... I REMEMBER I GOT A **PLASTIC CANTEEN** FOR A PRIZE!
MY DAD MUST HAVE PICKED THAT OUT...
OH **CUTE!** LOOK AT ME!
WHAT A LITTLE **HOSEBAG!**
SHUT UP! I WAS TOTALLY **ADORABLE!**
GOD, I REMEMBER THAT RECORD -- I USED TO PLAY THAT LIKE A **HUNDRED TIMES** EVERY DAY!
♫ I'VE GOT A SMILE ON MY FACE AND A RI-BBON SOMETHING SOMETHING
♫ ...A RI-BBON FOR MY HAIR... ♫
A SMILE AND
...I CAN'T REMEMBER, BUT IT WAS TOTALLY AMAZING!
WHATEVER HAPPENED TO ALL MY OLD RECORDS?
TSK!
CLACK CLACK
CLACK CLACK
CLACK CLACK CLACK
GOD, NO WONDER KIDS ARE SO SCREWED-UP TODAY -- THESE CHILDREN'S RECORDS ARE TOTALLY **CREEPY!** THIS GUY LOOKS LIKE A **CHILD MOLESTER!**
YOU'LL NEVER FIND IT HERE...
REN'S IC
Banana Club
IF I DON'T FIND THAT RECORD I'LL BE LACHRYMOSE!
YOU'LL WHAT?
OH SHIT!!

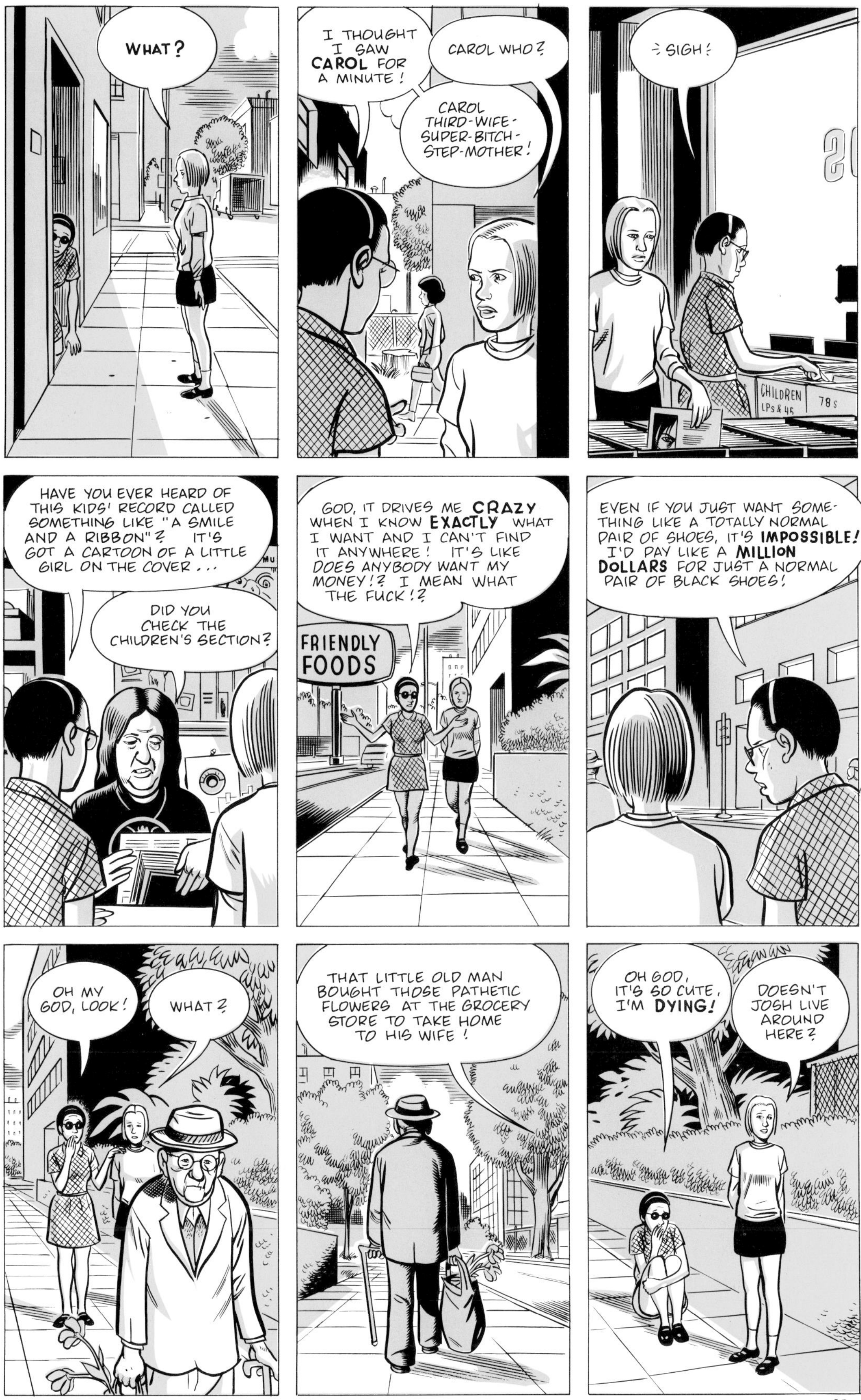
WHAT?
I THOUGHT I SAW CAROL FOR A MINUTE!
CAROL WHO?
CAROL THIRD-WIFE-SUPER-BITCH-STEP-MOTHER!
SIGH
CHILDREN LPs & 45
78s
HAVE YOU EVER HEARD OF THIS KIDS' RECORD CALLED SOMETHING LIKE "A SMILE AND A RIBBON"? IT'S GOT A CARTOON OF A LITTLE GIRL ON THE COVER...
DID YOU CHECK THE CHILDREN'S SECTION?
GOD, IT DRIVES ME CRAZY WHEN I KNOW EXACTLY WHAT I WANT AND I CAN'T FIND IT ANYWHERE! IT'S LIKE DOES ANYBODY WANT MY MONEY!? I MEAN WHAT THE FUCK!?
FRIENDLY FOODS
EVEN IF YOU JUST WANT SOMETHING LIKE A TOTALLY NORMAL PAIR OF SHOES, IT'S IMPOSSIBLE! I'D PAY LIKE A MILLION DOLLARS FOR JUST A NORMAL PAIR OF BLACK SHOES!
OH MY GOD, LOOK!
WHAT?
THAT LITTLE OLD MAN BOUGHT THOSE PATHETIC FLOWERS AT THE GROCERY STORE TO TAKE HOME TO HIS WIFE!
OH GOD, IT'S SO CUTE, I'M DYING!
DOESN'T JOSH LIVE AROUND HERE?

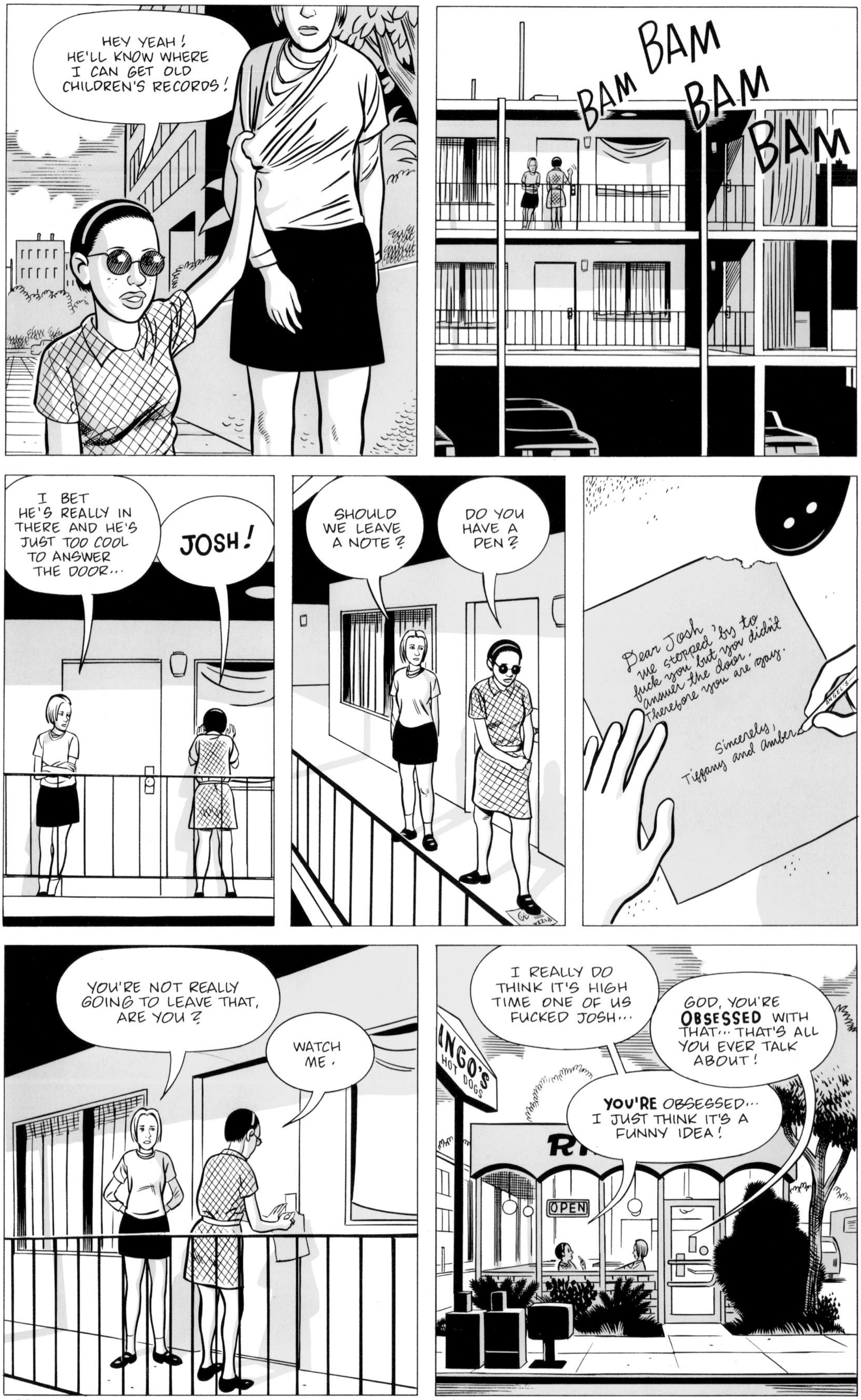
HEY YEAH! HE'LL KNOW WHERE I CAN GET OLD CHILDREN'S RECORDS!
BAM BAM BAM BAM
I BET HE'S REALLY IN THERE AND HE'S JUST TOO COOL TO ANSWER THE DOOR...
JOSH!
SHOULD WE LEAVE A NOTE?
DO YOU HAVE A PEN?
Dear Josh,
we stopped by to fuck you but you didn't answer the door.
Therefore you are gay.
Sincerely,
Tiffany and Amber
YOU'RE NOT REALLY GOING TO LEAVE THAT, ARE YOU?
WATCH ME.
I REALLY DO THINK IT'S HIGH TIME ONE OF US FUCKED JOSH...
GOD, YOU'RE OBSESSED WITH THAT... THAT'S ALL YOU EVER TALK ABOUT!
YOU'RE OBSESSED... I JUST THINK IT'S A FUNNY IDEA!
HOT DOGS
OPEN

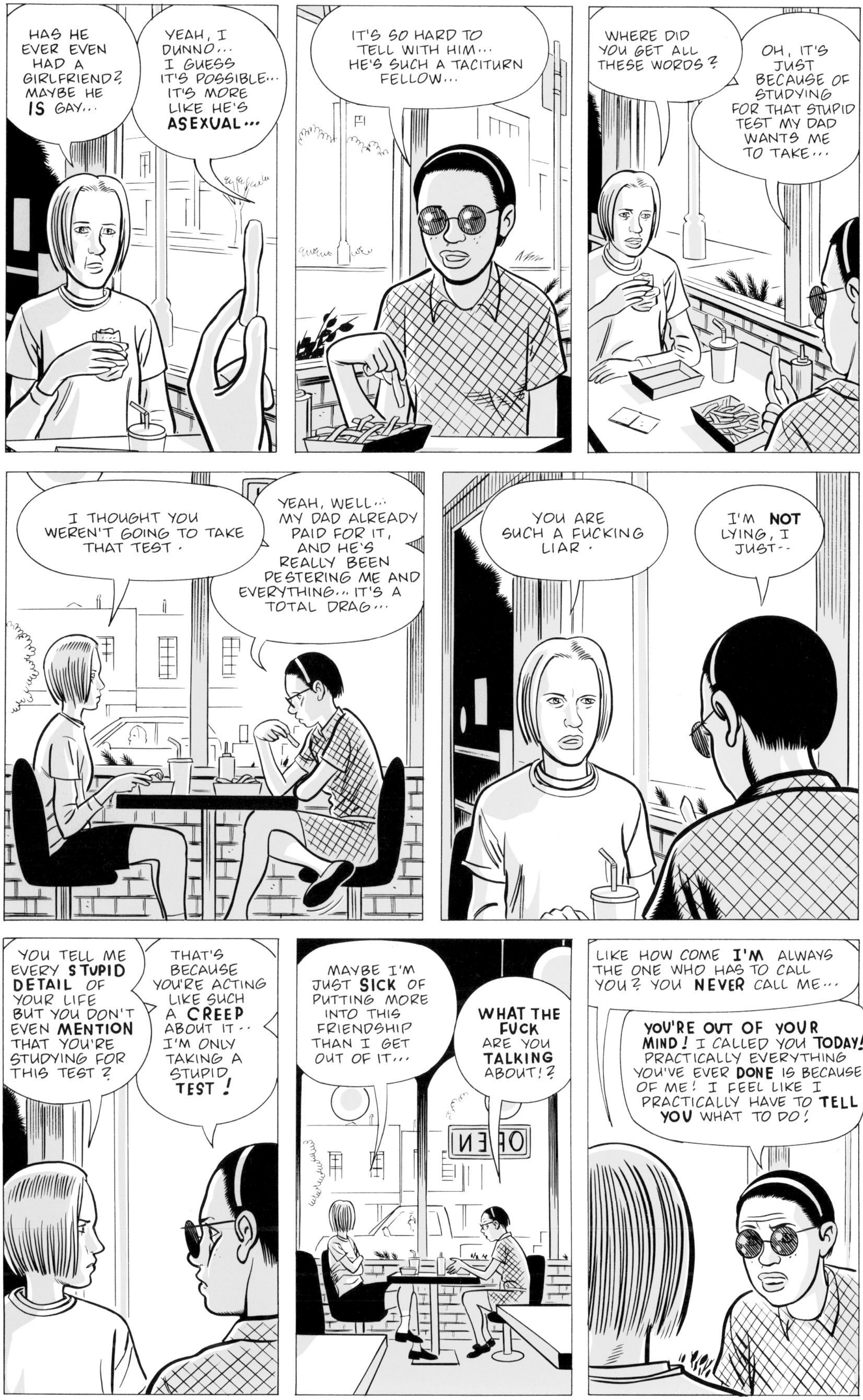
HAS HE EVER EVEN HAD A GIRLFRIEND? MAYBE HE IS GAY...
YEAH, I DUNNO... I GUESS IT'S POSSIBLE... IT'S MORE LIKE HE'S ASEXUAL...
IT'S SO HARD TO TELL WITH HIM... HE'S SUCH A TACITURN FELLOW...
WHERE DID YOU GET ALL THESE WORDS?
OH, IT'S JUST BECAUSE OF STUDYING FOR THAT STUPID TEST MY DAD WANTS ME TO TAKE...
I THOUGHT YOU WEREN'T GOING TO TAKE THAT TEST.
YEAH, WELL... MY DAD ALREADY PAID FOR IT, AND HE'S REALLY BEEN PESTERING ME AND EVERYTHING... IT'S A TOTAL DRAG...
YOU ARE SUCH A FUCKING LIAR.
I'M NOT LYING, I JUST--
YOU TELL ME EVERY STUPID DETAIL OF YOUR LIFE BUT YOU DON'T EVEN MENTION THAT YOU'RE STUDYING FOR THIS TEST?
THAT'S BECAUSE YOU'RE ACTING LIKE SUCH A CREEP ABOUT IT.. I'M ONLY TAKING A STUPID TEST!
MAYBE I'M JUST SICK OF PUTTING MORE INTO THIS FRIENDSHIP THAN I GET OUT OF IT...
WHAT THE FUCK ARE YOU TALKING ABOUT!?
OPEN
LIKE HOW COME I'M ALWAYS THE ONE WHO HAS TO CALL YOU? YOU NEVER CALL ME...
YOU'RE OUT OF YOUR MIND! I CALLED YOU TODAY! PRACTICALLY EVERYTHING YOU'VE EVER DONE IS BECAUSE OF ME! I FEEL LIKE I PRACTICALLY HAVE TO TELL YOU WHAT TO DO!

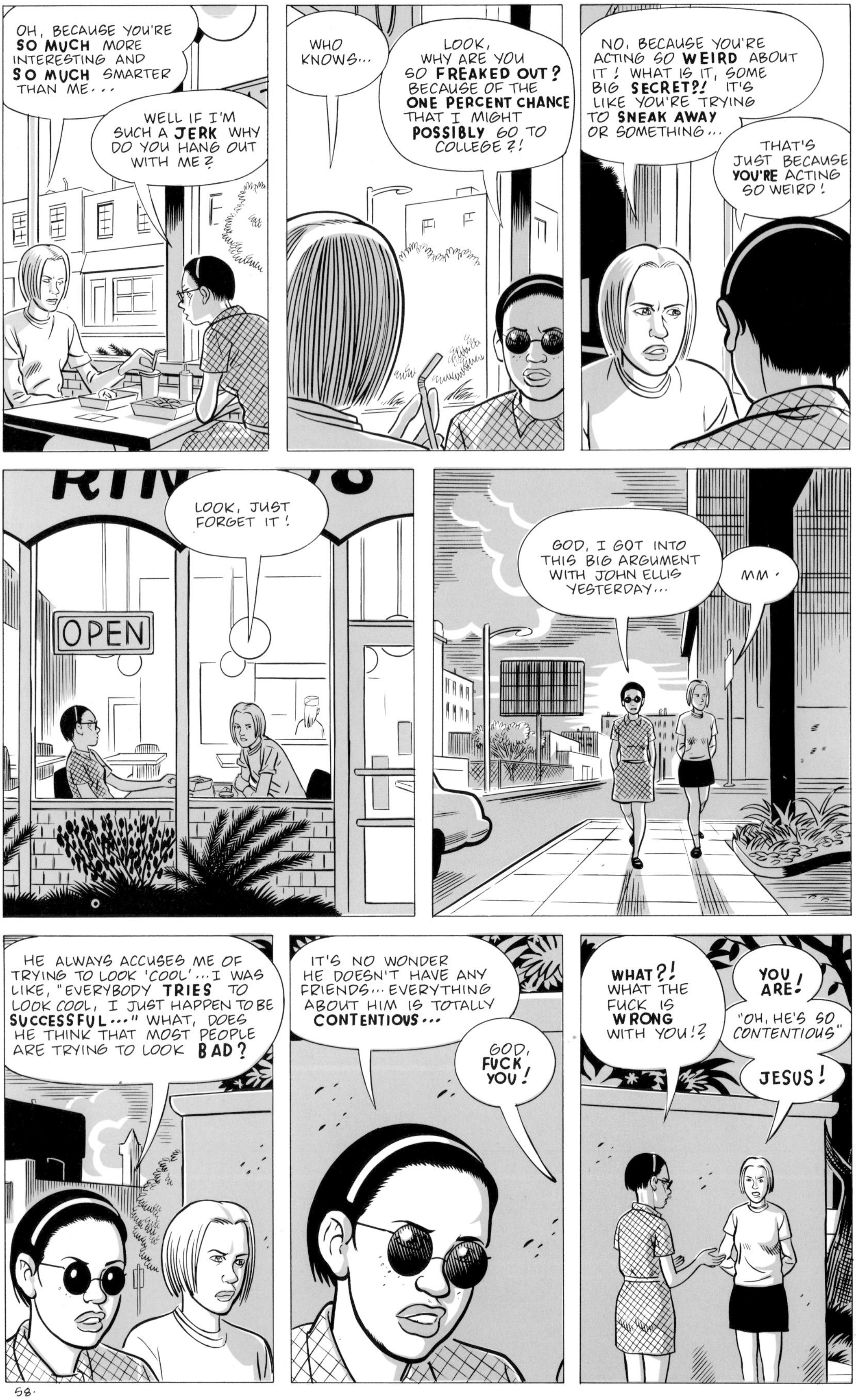
OH, BECAUSE YOU'RE SO MUCH MORE INTERESTING AND SO MUCH SMARTER THAN ME...
WELL IF I'M SUCH A JERK WHY DO YOU HANG OUT WITH ME?
WHO KNOWS...
LOOK, WHY ARE YOU SO FREAKED OUT? BECAUSE OF THE ONE PERCENT CHANCE THAT I MIGHT POSSIBLY GO TO COLLEGE?!
NO, BECAUSE YOU'RE ACTING SO WEIRD ABOUT IT! WHAT IS IT, SOME BIG SECRET?! IT'S LIKE YOU'RE TRYING TO SNEAK AWAY OR SOMETHING...
THAT'S JUST BECAUSE YOU'RE ACTING SO WEIRD!
OPEN
LOOK, JUST FORGET IT!
GOD, I GOT INTO THIS BIG ARGUMENT WITH JOHN ELLIS YESTERDAY...
MM.
HE ALWAYS ACCUSES ME OF TRYING TO LOOK 'COOL'... I WAS LIKE, "EVERYBODY TRIES TO LOOK COOL, I JUST HAPPEN TO BE SUCCESSFUL..." WHAT, DOES HE THINK THAT MOST PEOPLE ARE TRYING TO LOOK BAD?
IT'S NO WONDER HE DOESN'T HAVE ANY FRIENDS... EVERYTHING ABOUT HIM IS TOTALLY CONTENTIOUS...
GOD, FUCK YOU!
WHAT?! WHAT THE FUCK IS WRONG WITH YOU!?
YOU ARE!
"OH, HE'S SO CONTENTIOUS"
JESUS!

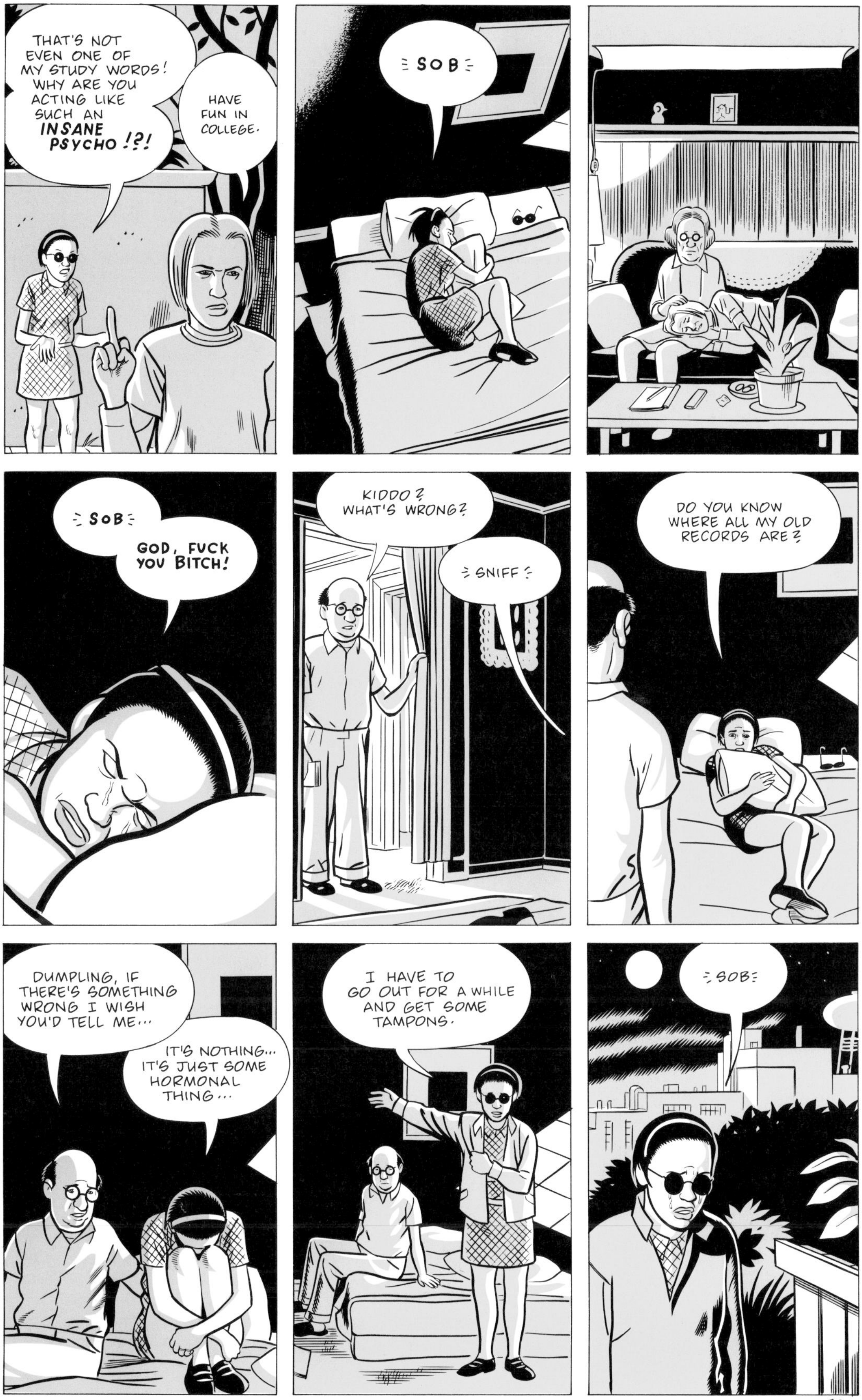
THAT'S NOT EVEN ONE OF MY STUDY WORDS! WHY ARE YOU ACTING LIKE SUCH AN INSANE PSYCHO!?!
HAVE FUN IN COLLEGE.
SOB
SOB
GOD, FUCK YOU BITCH!
KIDDO? WHAT'S WRONG?
SNIFF
DO YOU KNOW WHERE ALL MY OLD RECORDS ARE?
DUMPLING, IF THERE'S SOMETHING WRONG I WISH YOU'D TELL ME...
IT'S NOTHING... IT'S JUST SOME HORMONAL THING...
I HAVE TO GO OUT FOR A WHILE AND GET SOME TAMPONS.
SOB

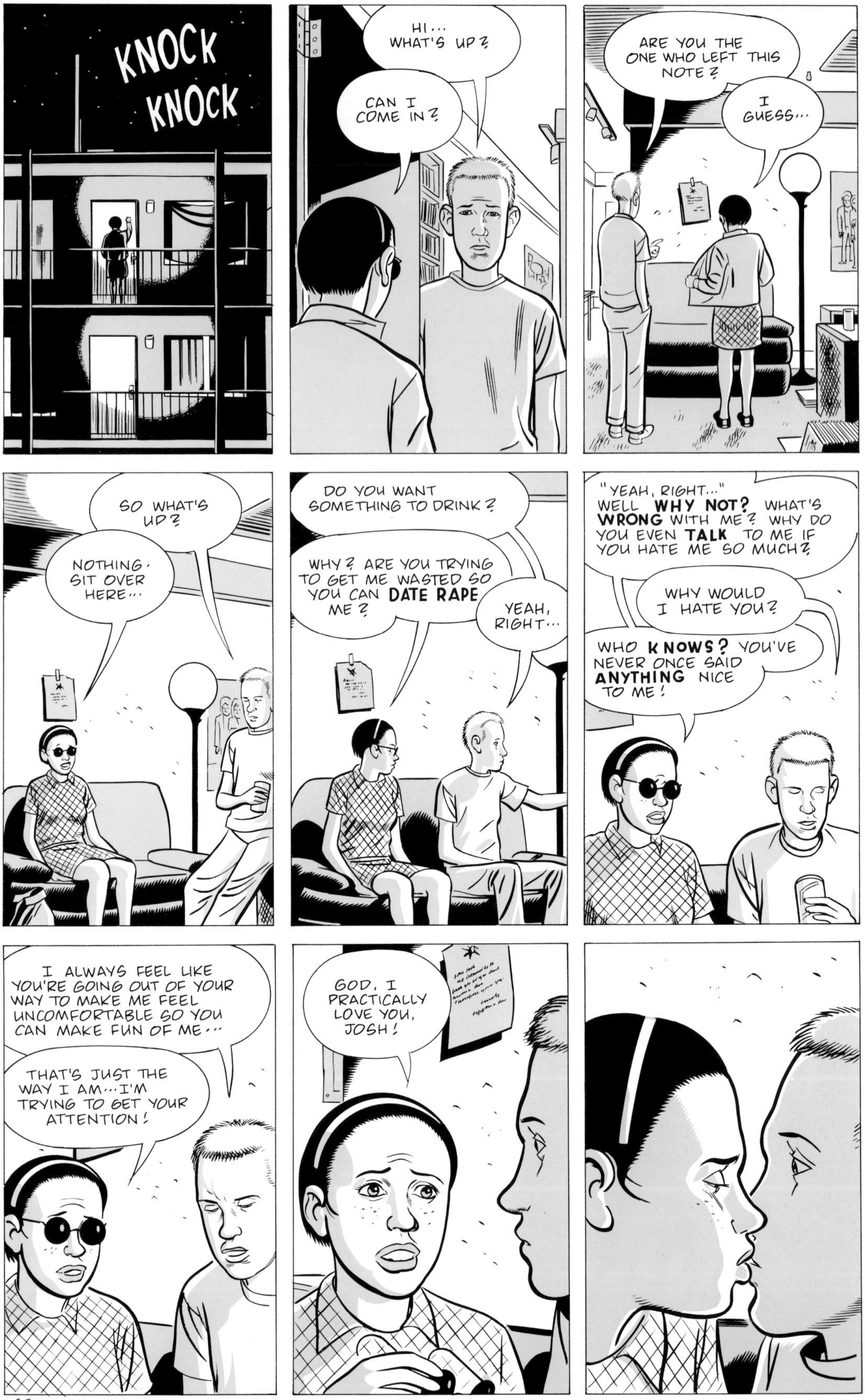
KNOCK KNOCK
HI... WHAT'S UP?
CAN I COME IN?
ARE YOU THE ONE WHO LEFT THIS NOTE?
I GUESS...
SO WHAT'S UP?
NOTHING. SIT OVER HERE...
DO YOU WANT SOMETHING TO DRINK?
WHY? ARE YOU TRYING TO GET ME WASTED SO YOU CAN DATE RAPE ME?
YEAH, RIGHT...
"YEAH, RIGHT..." WELL WHY NOT? WHAT'S WRONG WITH ME? WHY DO YOU EVEN TALK TO ME IF YOU HATE ME SO MUCH?
WHY WOULD I HATE YOU?
WHO KNOWS? YOU'VE NEVER ONCE SAID ANYTHING NICE TO ME!
I ALWAYS FEEL LIKE YOU'RE GOING OUT OF YOUR WAY TO MAKE ME FEEL UNCOMFORTABLE SO YOU CAN MAKE FUN OF ME...
THAT'S JUST THE WAY I AM... I'M TRYING TO GET YOUR ATTENTION!
GOD, I PRACTICALLY LOVE YOU, JOSH!

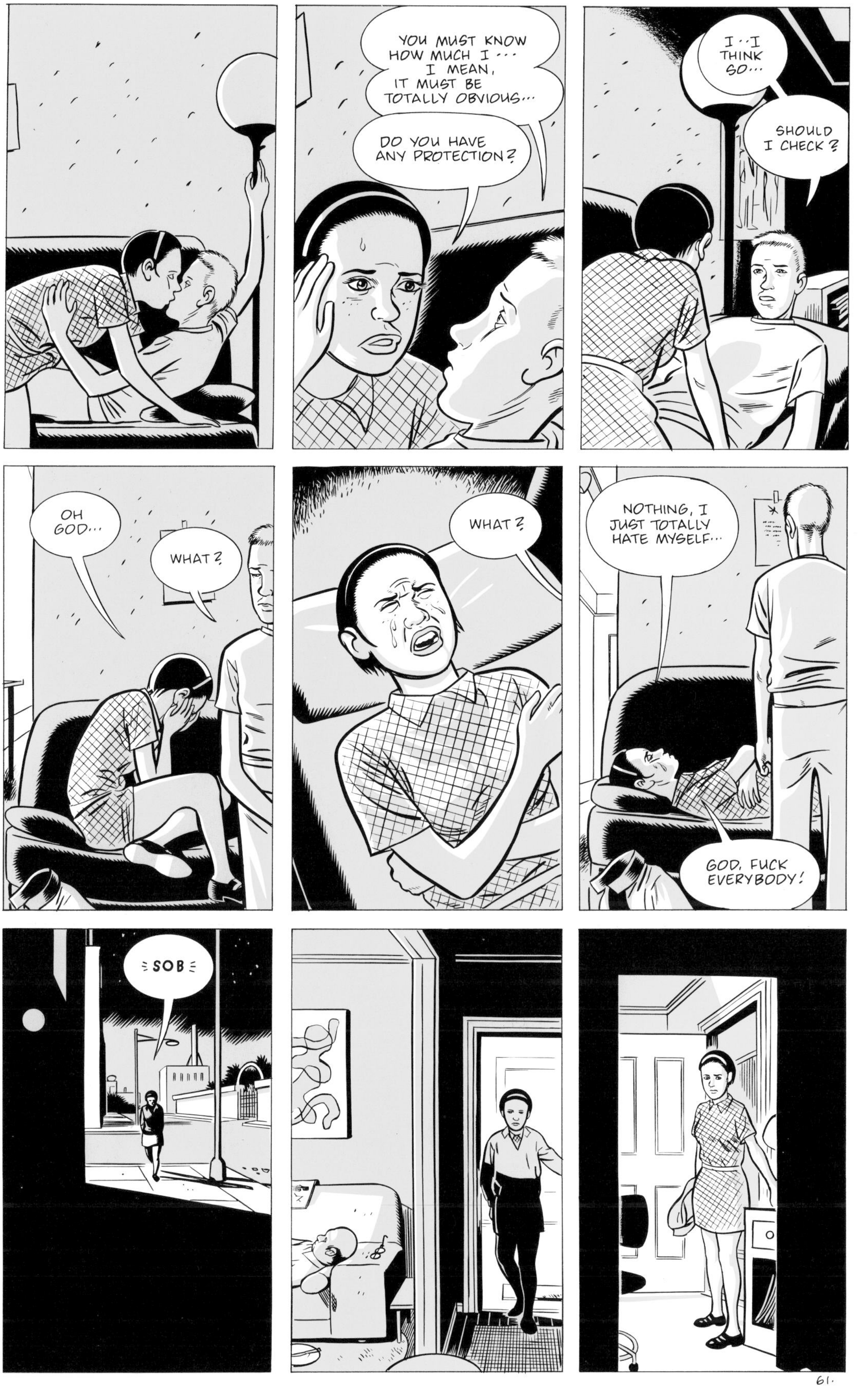
YOU MUST KNOW HOW MUCH I ··· I MEAN,
IT MUST BE TOTALLY OBVIOUS...
DO YOU HAVE ANY PROTECTION?
I··I THINK SO...
SHOULD I CHECK?
OH GOD...
WHAT?
WHAT?
NOTHING, I JUST TOTALLY HATE MYSELF...
GOD, FUCK EVERYBODY!
SOB

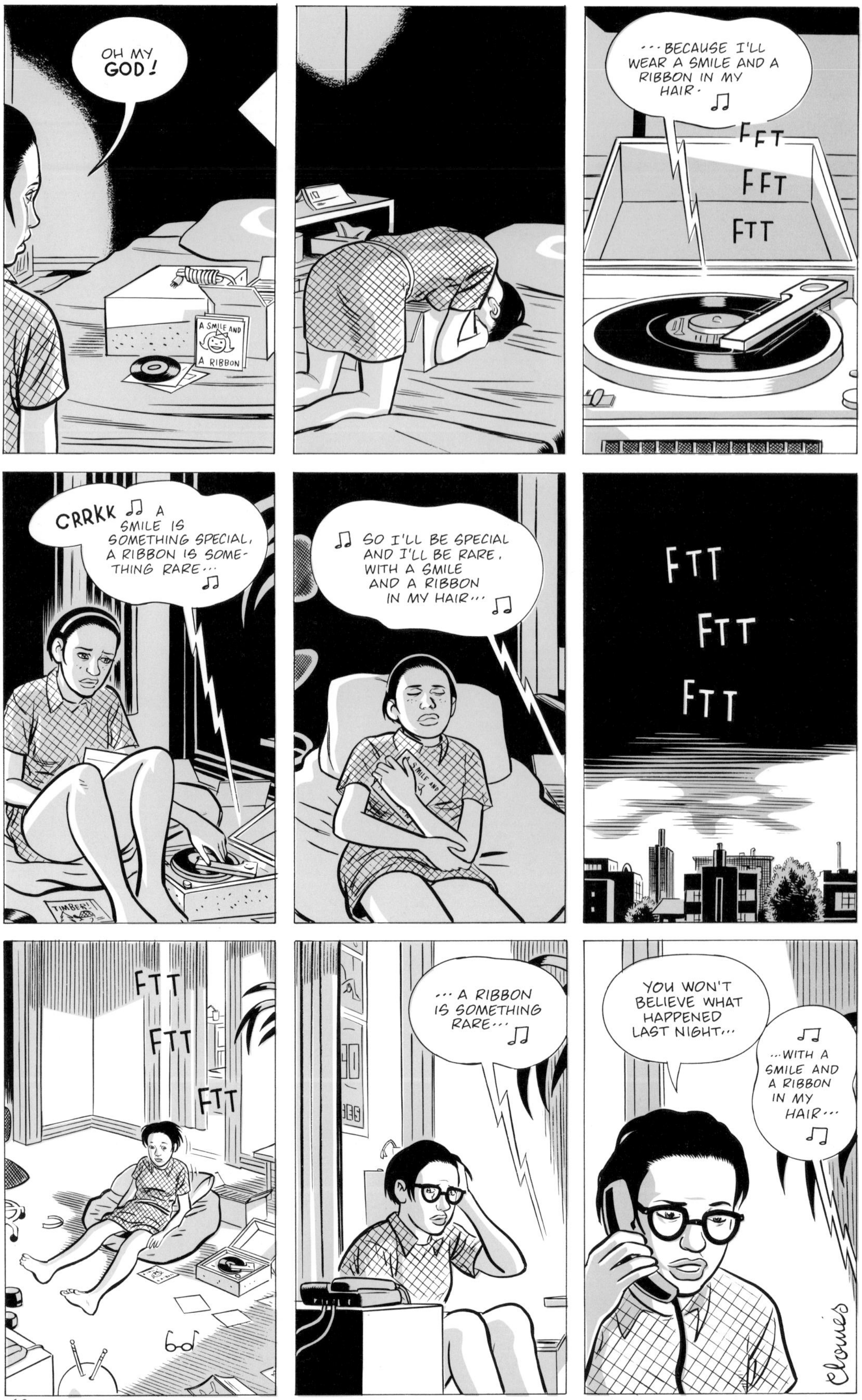
OH MY GOD!
A SMILE AND A RIBBON
...BECAUSE I'LL WEAR A SMILE AND A RIBBON IN MY HAIR. ♫
FFT
FFT
FTT
CRRKK ♫ A SMILE IS SOMETHING SPECIAL, A RIBBON IS SOME-THING RARE... ♫
TIMBER!
♫ SO I'LL BE SPECIAL AND I'LL BE RARE, WITH A SMILE AND A RIBBON IN MY HAIR... ♫
SMILE AND
FTT
FTT
FTT
FTT
FTT
FTT
...A RIBBON IS SOMETHING RARE... ♫
YOU WON'T BELIEVE WHAT HAPPENED LAST NIGHT...
♫ ...WITH A SMILE AND A RIBBON IN MY HAIR... ♫
clowes

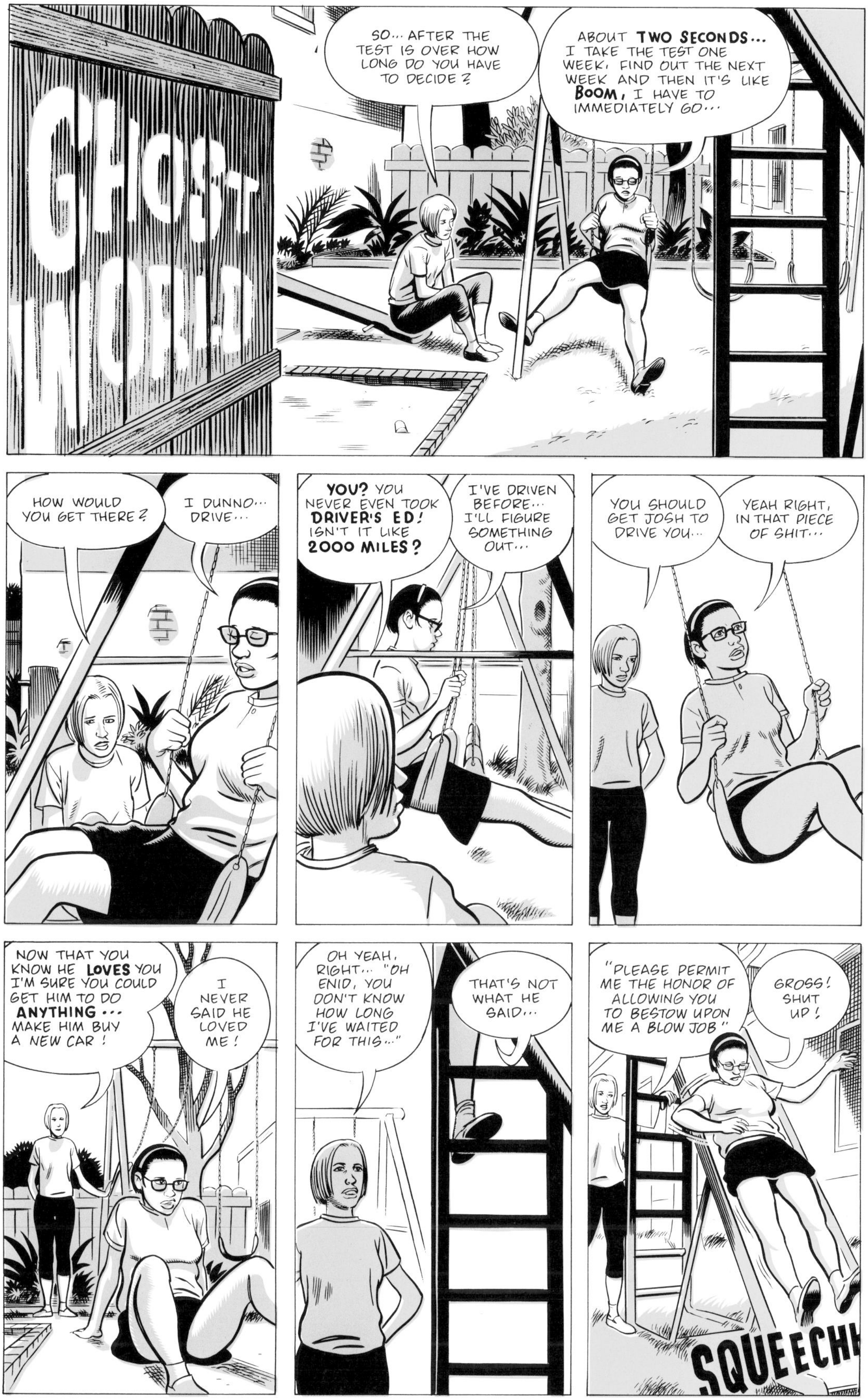
GHOST WORLD
SO... AFTER THE TEST IS OVER HOW LONG DO YOU HAVE TO DECIDE?
ABOUT TWO SECONDS... I TAKE THE TEST ONE WEEK, FIND OUT THE NEXT WEEK AND THEN IT'S LIKE BOOM, I HAVE TO IMMEDIATELY GO...
HOW WOULD YOU GET THERE?
I DUNNO... DRIVE...
YOU? YOU NEVER EVEN TOOK DRIVER'S ED! ISN'T IT LIKE 2000 MILES?
I'VE DRIVEN BEFORE... I'LL FIGURE SOMETHING OUT...
YOU SHOULD GET JOSH TO DRIVE YOU...
YEAH RIGHT, IN THAT PIECE OF SHIT...
NOW THAT YOU KNOW HE LOVES YOU I'M SURE YOU COULD GET HIM TO DO ANYTHING... MAKE HIM BUY A NEW CAR!
I NEVER SAID HE LOVED ME!
OH YEAH, RIGHT... "OH ENID, YOU DON'T KNOW HOW LONG I'VE WAITED FOR THIS..."
THAT'S NOT WHAT HE SAID...
"PLEASE PERMIT ME THE HONOR OF ALLOWING YOU TO BESTOW UPON ME A BLOW JOB"
GROSS! SHUT UP!
SQUEECHH

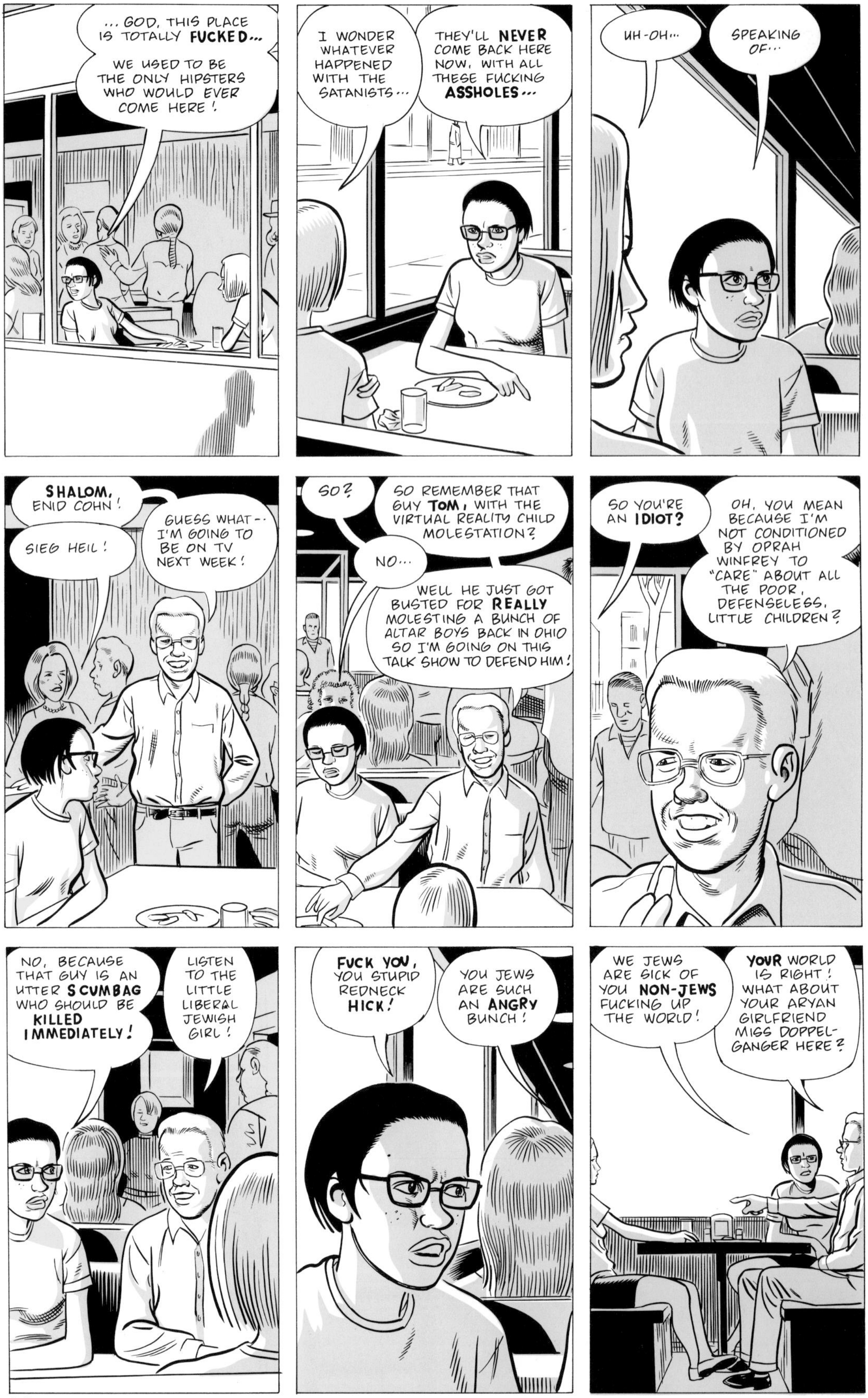

... GOD, THIS PLACE IS TOTALLY FUCKED...
WE USED TO BE THE ONLY HIPSTERS WHO WOULD EVER COME HERE!
I WONDER WHATEVER HAPPENED WITH THE SATANISTS...
THEY'LL NEVER COME BACK HERE NOW, WITH ALL THESE FUCKING ASSHOLES...
UH-OH...
SPEAKING OF...
SHALOM, ENID COHN!
SIEG HEIL!
GUESS WHAT-- I'M GOING TO BE ON TV NEXT WEEK!
SO?
SO REMEMBER THAT GUY TOM, WITH THE VIRTUAL REALITY CHILD MOLESTATION?
NO...
WELL HE JUST GOT BUSTED FOR REALLY MOLESTING A BUNCH OF ALTAR BOYS BACK IN OHIO SO I'M GOING ON THIS TALK SHOW TO DEFEND HIM!
SO YOU'RE AN IDIOT?
OH, YOU MEAN BECAUSE I'M NOT CONDITIONED BY OPRAH WINFREY TO "CARE" ABOUT ALL THE POOR, DEFENSELESS, LITTLE CHILDREN?
NO, BECAUSE THAT GUY IS AN UTTER SCUMBAG WHO SHOULD BE KILLED IMMEDIATELY!
LISTEN TO THE LITTLE LIBERAL JEWISH GIRL!
FUCK YOU, YOU STUPID REDNECK HICK!
YOU JEWS ARE SUCH AN ANGRY BUNCH!
WE JEWS ARE SICK OF YOU NON-JEWS FUCKING UP THE WORLD!
YOUR WORLD IS RIGHT! WHAT ABOUT YOUR ARYAN GIRLFRIEND MISS DOPPEL-GANGER HERE?

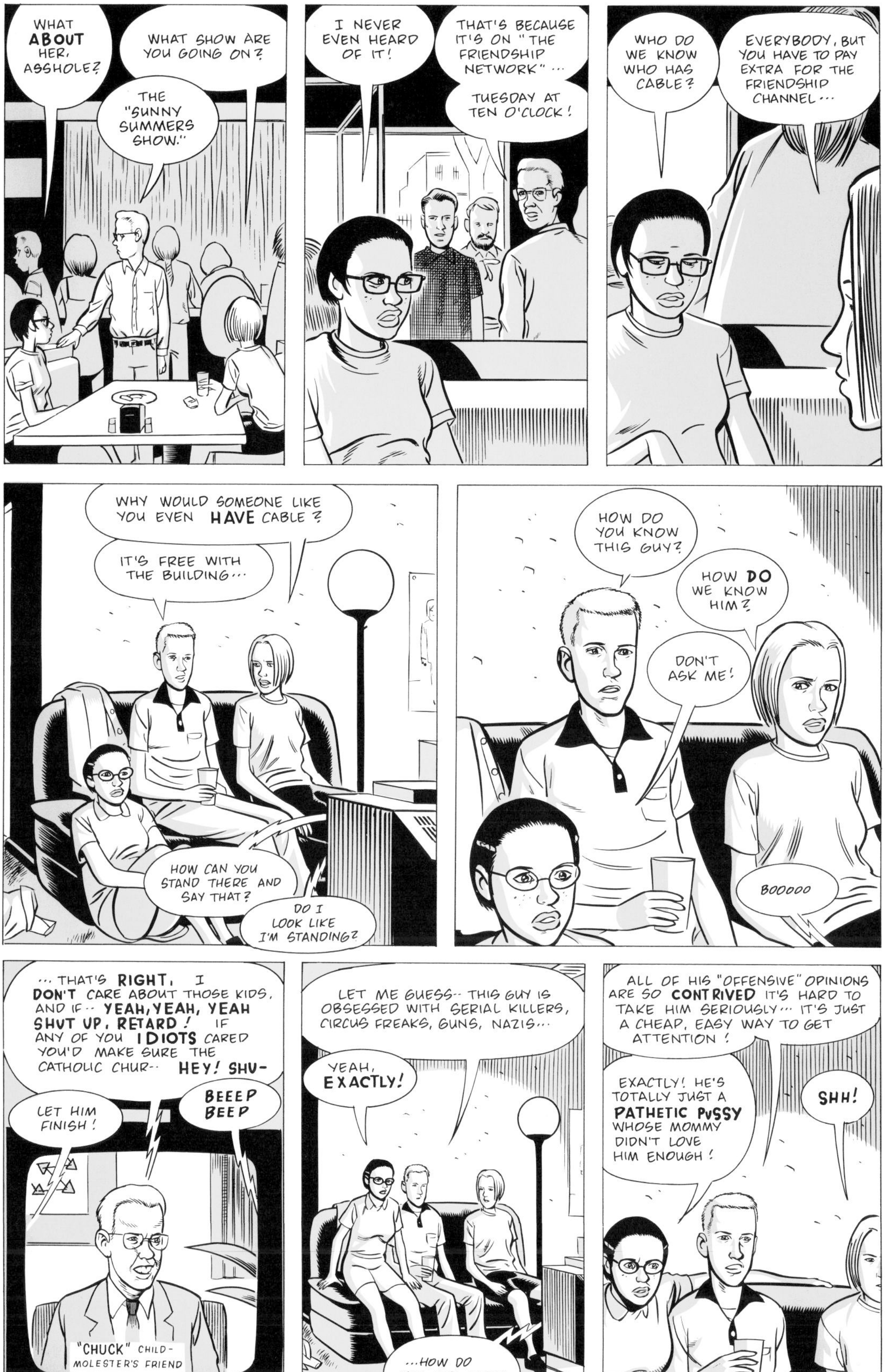
WHAT ABOUT HER, ASSHOLE?
WHAT SHOW ARE YOU GOING ON?
THE "SUNNY SUMMERS SHOW."
I NEVER EVEN HEARD OF IT!
THAT'S BECAUSE IT'S ON "THE FRIENDSHIP NETWORK"...
TUESDAY AT TEN O'CLOCK!
WHO DO WE KNOW WHO HAS CABLE?
EVERYBODY, BUT YOU HAVE TO PAY EXTRA FOR THE FRIENDSHIP CHANNEL...
WHY WOULD SOMEONE LIKE YOU EVEN HAVE CABLE?
IT'S FREE WITH THE BUILDING...
HOW CAN YOU STAND THERE AND SAY THAT?
DO I LOOK LIKE I'M STANDING?
HOW DO YOU KNOW THIS GUY?
HOW DO WE KNOW HIM?
DON'T ASK ME!
BOOOOO
...THAT'S RIGHT, I DON'T CARE ABOUT THOSE KIDS, AND IF-- YEAH, YEAH, YEAH SHUT UP, RETARD! IF ANY OF YOU IDIOTS CARED YOU'D MAKE SURE THE CATHOLIC CHUR-- HEY! SHU-
LET HIM FINISH!
BEEEP BEEP
"CHUCK" CHILD-MOLESTER'S FRIEND
LET ME GUESS-- THIS GUY IS OBSESSED WITH SERIAL KILLERS, CIRCUS FREAKS, GUNS, NAZIS...
YEAH, EXACTLY!
...HOW DO YOU FEEL ABOUT HIM?
ALL OF HIS "OFFENSIVE" OPINIONS ARE SO CONTRIVED IT'S HARD TO TAKE HIM SERIOUSLY... IT'S JUST A CHEAP, EASY WAY TO GET ATTENTION!
EXACTLY! HE'S TOTALLY JUST A PATHETIC PUSSY WHOSE MOMMY DIDN'T LOVE HIM ENOUGH!
SHH!

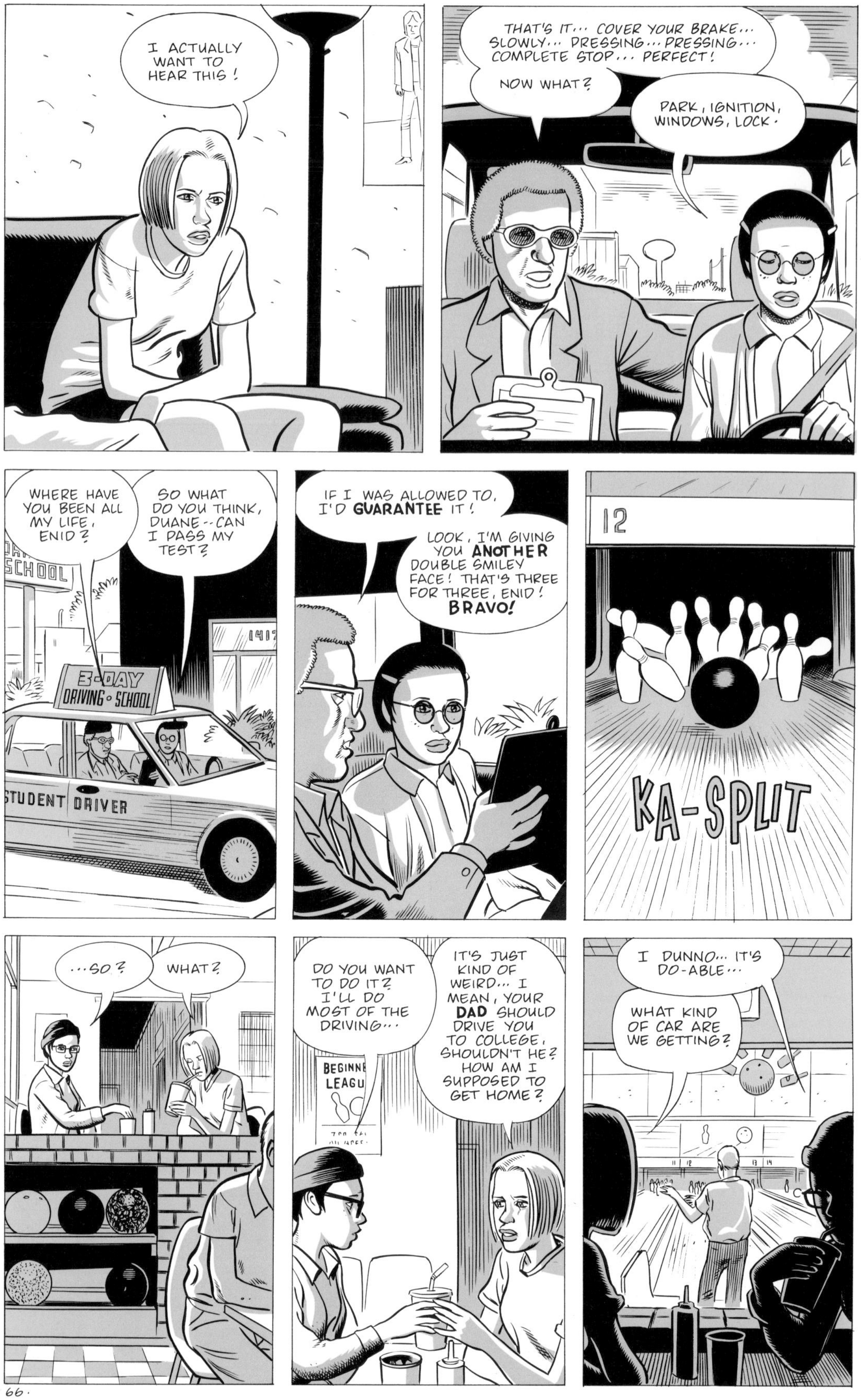
I ACTUALLY WANT TO HEAR THIS!
THAT'S IT... COVER YOUR BRAKE... SLOWLY... PRESSING... PRESSING... COMPLETE STOP... PERFECT!
NOW WHAT?
PARK, IGNITION, WINDOWS, LOCK.
WHERE HAVE YOU BEEN ALL MY LIFE, ENID?
SO WHAT DO YOU THINK, DUANE--CAN I PASS MY TEST?
3-DAY DRIVING SCHOOL
STUDENT DRIVER
IF I WAS ALLOWED TO, I'D GUARANTEE IT!
LOOK, I'M GIVING YOU ANOTHER DOUBLE SMILEY FACE! THAT'S THREE FOR THREE, ENID! BRAVO!
12
KA-SPLIT
...SO?
WHAT?
DO YOU WANT TO DO IT? I'LL DO MOST OF THE DRIVING...
IT'S JUST KIND OF WEIRD... I MEAN, YOUR DAD SHOULD DRIVE YOU TO COLLEGE, SHOULDN'T HE? HOW AM I SUPPOSED TO GET HOME?
I DUNNO... IT'S DO-ABLE...
WHAT KIND OF CAR ARE WE GETTING?

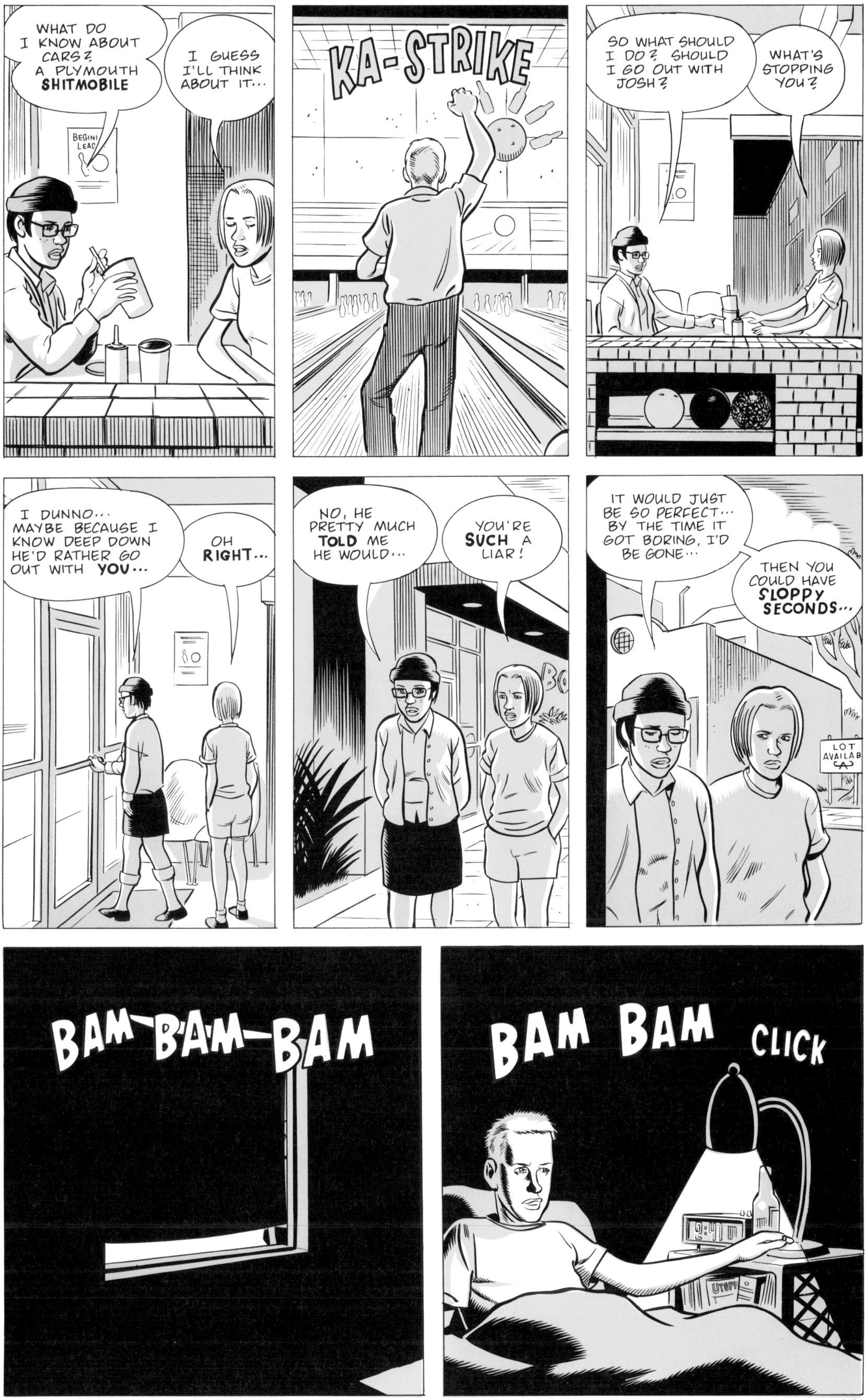
WHAT DO I KNOW ABOUT CARS? A PLYMOUTH **SHITMOBILE**
I GUESS I'LL THINK ABOUT IT...
KA-STRIKE
SO WHAT SHOULD I DO? SHOULD I GO OUT WITH JOSH?
WHAT'S STOPPING YOU?
I DUNNO... MAYBE BECAUSE I KNOW DEEP DOWN HE'D RATHER GO OUT WITH **YOU**...
OH **RIGHT**...
NO, HE PRETTY MUCH **TOLD** ME HE WOULD...
YOU'RE **SUCH** A LIAR!
IT WOULD JUST BE SO PERFECT... BY THE TIME IT GOT BORING, I'D BE GONE...
THEN YOU COULD HAVE **SLOPPY SECONDS**...
BAM-BAM-BAM
BAM BAM
CLICK

HI.
WHAT ARE YOU UP TO?

LIKE I SAID, THESE THINGS ARE GETTIN' HARDER TO FIND; NOW THEY USE VANS, I THINK···; BUT YOU COULD DO A LOT WORSE THAN THIS ONE, ESPECIALLY FOR A NEW DRIVER. SHE'S GOT UNBELIEVABLY LOW MILEAGE, AND IF YOU GET INTO AN ACCIDENT I **PROMISE** YOU'LL BE THE ONE WALKING AWAY!

YOU REALLY SHOULD THINK ABOUT THIS, PUMPKIN···. IT'S LIABLE TO COST A LOT MORE THAN YOU THINK; YOU'RE GOING TO HAVE TO SPEND A **FORTUNE** ON GAS···

IT'S MY MONEY, ISN'T IT? CAN'T I DO WHAT I WANT JUST **ONCE** IN MY LIFE?

YOU'VE TRICKED ME INTO MOVING TWO THOUSAND MILES AWAY AND RUINING MY LIFE··· CAN'T YOU LET ME HAVE THIS ONE MORSEL OF FUN?

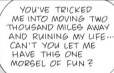

WHADDYA MEAN!? IT'S NOT "DEATH ROCK"! IT'S NOT EVEN **BLACK**!

I'M JUST SURPRISED··· IT'S NOT REALLY YOUR STYLE···

YOU DON'T KNOW ME, JOSH.

APPARENTLY NOT.

···SO WHAT **IS** MY STYLE?

TO DEFY DEFINITION··· CAN YOU LET ME OUT UP HERE AT THE PEPPER MILL···

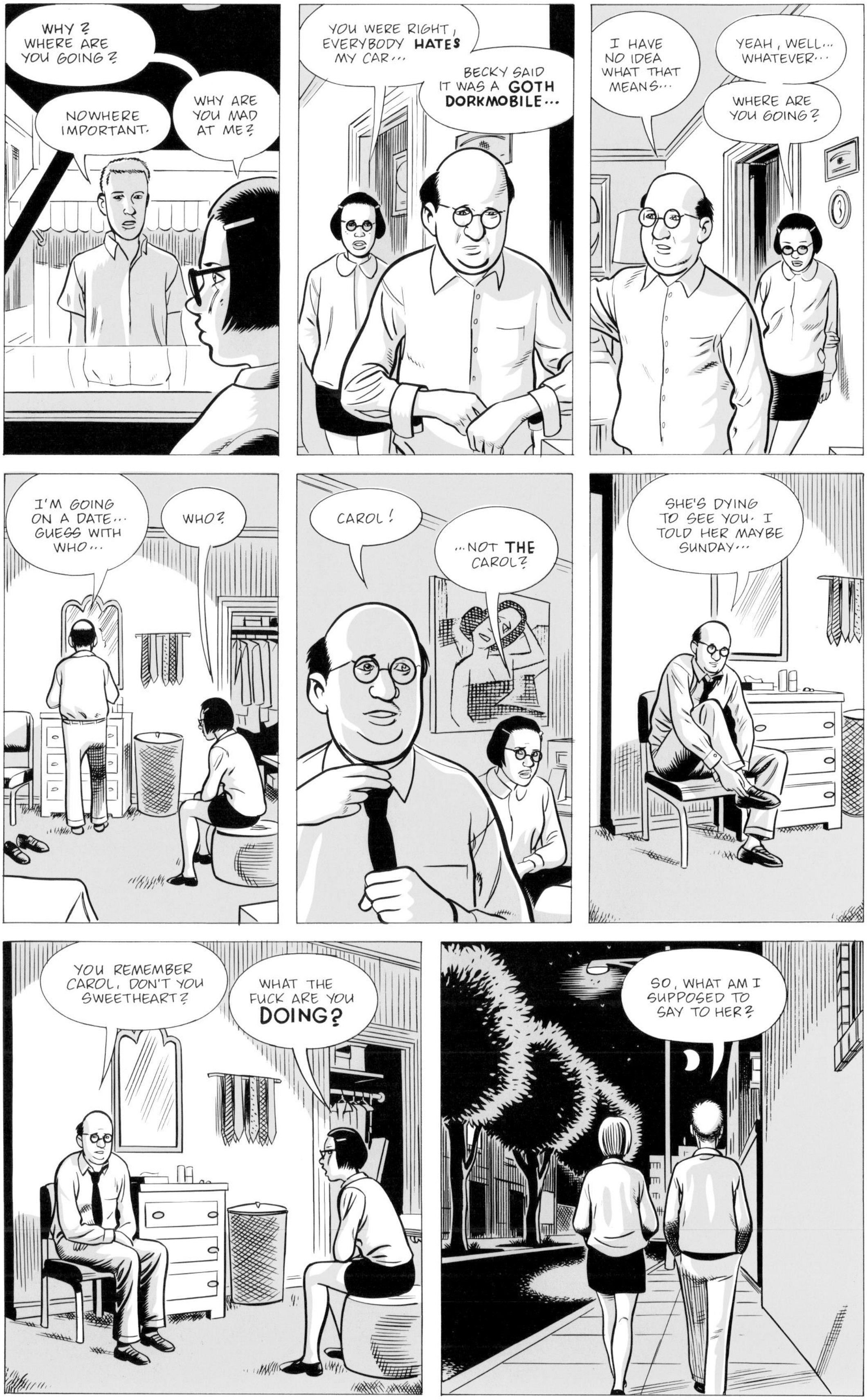
WHY? WHERE ARE YOU GOING?
NOWHERE IMPORTANT.
WHY ARE YOU MAD AT ME?
YOU WERE RIGHT, EVERYBODY **HATES** MY CAR...
BECKY SAID IT WAS A **GOTH DORKMOBILE**...
I HAVE NO IDEA WHAT THAT MEANS...
YEAH, WELL... WHATEVER...
WHERE ARE YOU GOING?
I'M GOING ON A DATE... GUESS WITH WHO...
WHO?
CAROL!
...NOT **THE** CAROL?
SHE'S DYING TO SEE YOU. I TOLD HER MAYBE SUNDAY...
YOU REMEMBER CAROL, DON'T YOU SWEETHEART?
WHAT THE FUCK ARE YOU **DOING?**
SO, WHAT AM I SUPPOSED TO SAY TO HER?

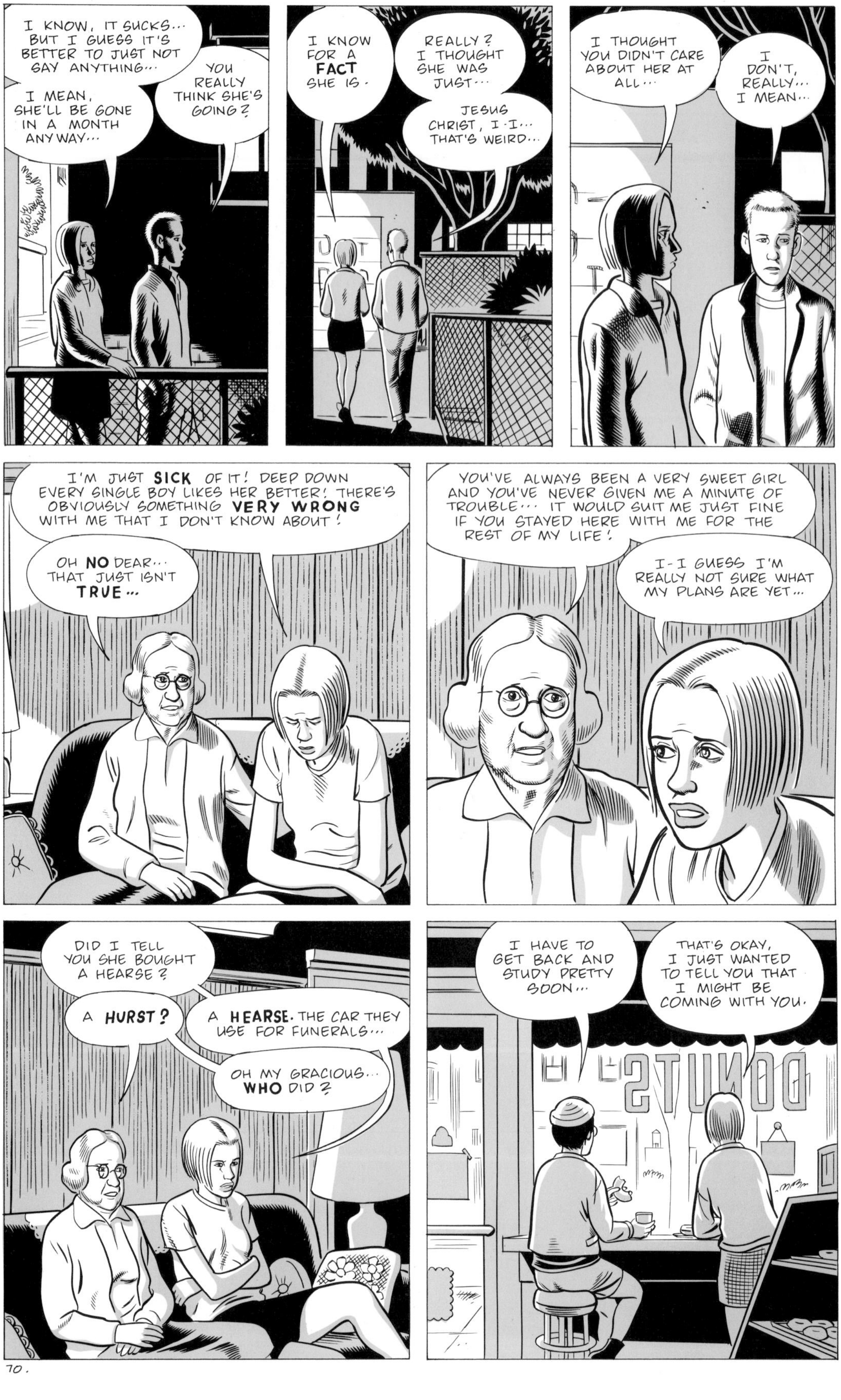
I KNOW, IT SUCKS... BUT I GUESS IT'S BETTER TO JUST NOT SAY ANYTHING...
I MEAN, SHE'LL BE GONE IN A MONTH ANYWAY...
YOU REALLY THINK SHE'S GOING?
I KNOW FOR A **FACT** SHE IS.
REALLY? I THOUGHT SHE WAS JUST...
JESUS CHRIST, I-I... THAT'S WEIRD...
I THOUGHT YOU DIDN'T CARE ABOUT HER AT ALL...
I DON'T, REALLY... I MEAN...
I'M JUST **SICK** OF IT! DEEP DOWN EVERY SINGLE BOY LIKES HER BETTER! THERE'S OBVIOUSLY SOMETHING **VERY WRONG** WITH ME THAT I DON'T KNOW ABOUT!
OH **NO** DEAR... THAT JUST ISN'T **TRUE**...
YOU'VE ALWAYS BEEN A VERY SWEET GIRL AND YOU'VE NEVER GIVEN ME A MINUTE OF TROUBLE... IT WOULD SUIT ME JUST FINE IF YOU STAYED HERE WITH ME FOR THE REST OF MY LIFE!
I-I GUESS I'M REALLY NOT SURE WHAT MY PLANS ARE YET...
DID I TELL YOU SHE BOUGHT A HEARSE?
A **HURST?**
A **HEARSE**. THE CAR THEY USE FOR FUNERALS...
OH MY GRACIOUS... **WHO** DID?
I HAVE TO GET BACK AND STUDY PRETTY SOON...
THAT'S OKAY, I JUST WANTED TO TELL YOU THAT I MIGHT BE COMING WITH YOU.

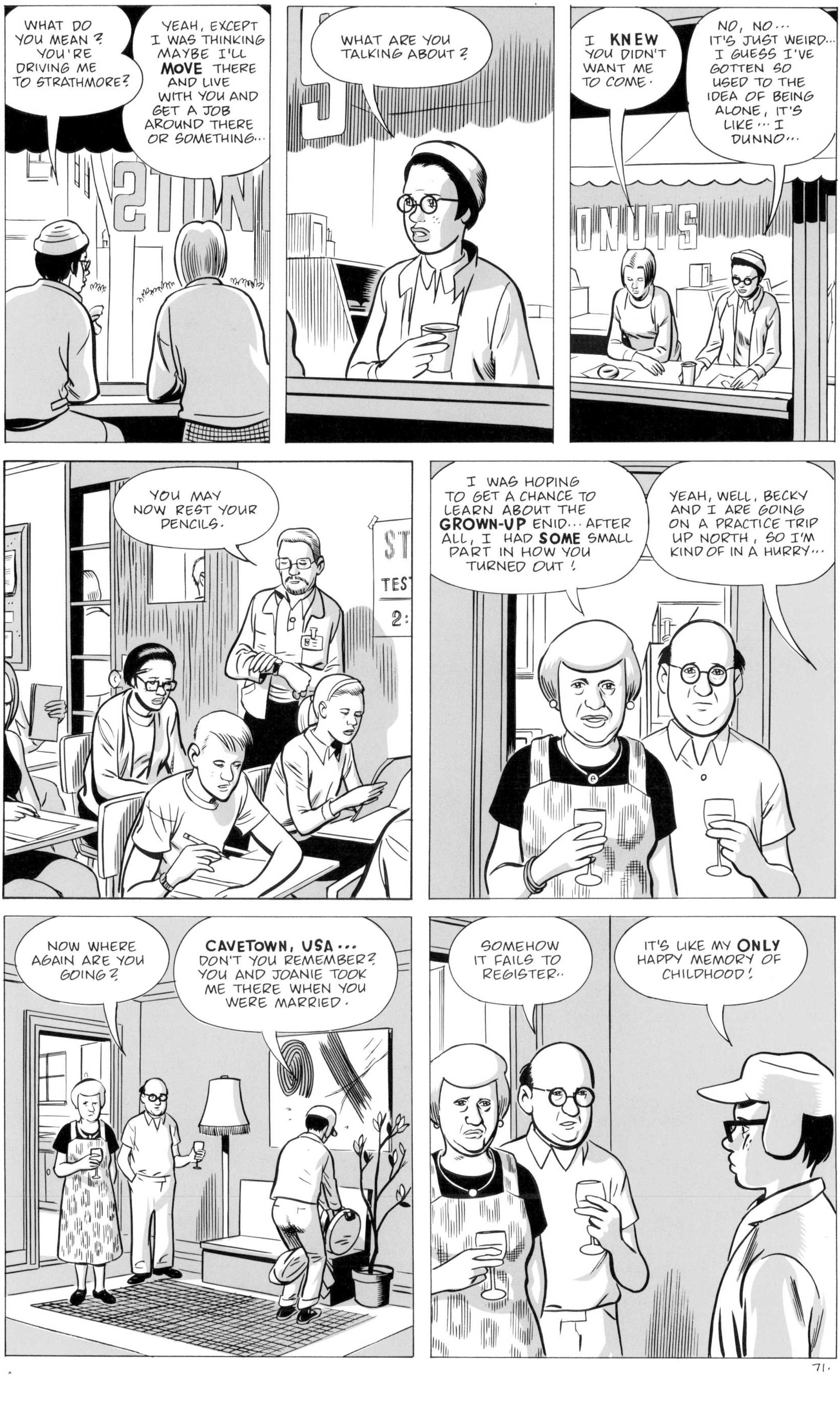
WHAT DO YOU MEAN? YOU'RE DRIVING ME TO STRATHMORE?
YEAH, EXCEPT I WAS THINKING MAYBE I'LL **MOVE** THERE AND LIVE WITH YOU AND GET A JOB AROUND THERE OR SOMETHING...
WHAT ARE YOU TALKING ABOUT?
I **KNEW** YOU DIDN'T WANT ME TO COME.
NO, NO... IT'S JUST WEIRD... I GUESS I'VE GOTTEN SO USED TO THE IDEA OF BEING ALONE, IT'S LIKE... I DUNNO...
YOU MAY NOW REST YOUR PENCILS.
I WAS HOPING TO GET A CHANCE TO LEARN ABOUT THE **GROWN-UP** ENID... AFTER ALL, I HAD **SOME** SMALL PART IN HOW YOU TURNED OUT!
YEAH, WELL, BECKY AND I ARE GOING ON A PRACTICE TRIP UP NORTH, SO I'M KIND OF IN A HURRY...
NOW WHERE AGAIN ARE YOU GOING?
CAVETOWN, USA... DON'T YOU REMEMBER? YOU AND JOANIE TOOK ME THERE WHEN YOU WERE MARRIED.
SOMEHOW IT FAILS TO REGISTER..
IT'S LIKE MY **ONLY** HAPPY MEMORY OF CHILDHOOD!

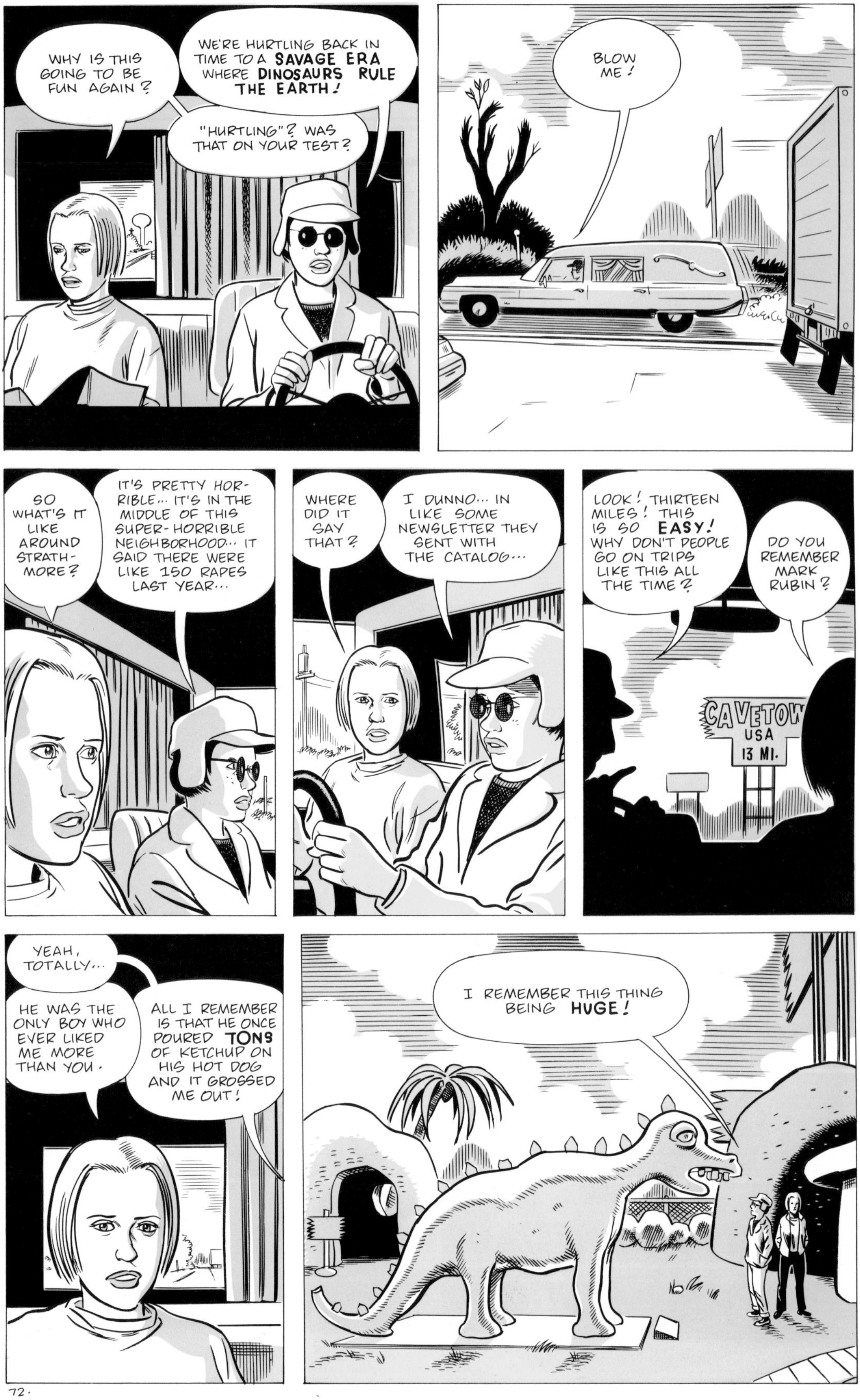
WHY IS THIS GOING TO BE FUN AGAIN?
WE'RE HURTLING BACK IN TIME TO A SAVAGE ERA WHERE DINOSAURS RULE THE EARTH!
"HURTLING"? WAS THAT ON YOUR TEST?
BLOW ME!
SO WHAT'S IT LIKE AROUND STRATH-MORE?
IT'S PRETTY HOR-RIBLE... IT'S IN THE MIDDLE OF THIS SUPER-HORRIBLE NEIGHBORHOOD... IT SAID THERE WERE LIKE 150 RAPES LAST YEAR...
WHERE DID IT SAY THAT?
I DUNNO... IN LIKE SOME NEWSLETTER THEY SENT WITH THE CATALOG...
LOOK! THIRTEEN MILES! THIS IS SO EASY! WHY DON'T PEOPLE GO ON TRIPS LIKE THIS ALL THE TIME?
DO YOU REMEMBER MARK RUBIN?
CAVETOW
USA
13 MI.
YEAH, TOTALLY...
HE WAS THE ONLY BOY WHO EVER LIKED ME MORE THAN YOU.
ALL I REMEMBER IS THAT HE ONCE POURED TONS OF KETCHUP ON HIS HOT DOG AND IT GROSSED ME OUT!
I REMEMBER THIS THING BEING HUGE!

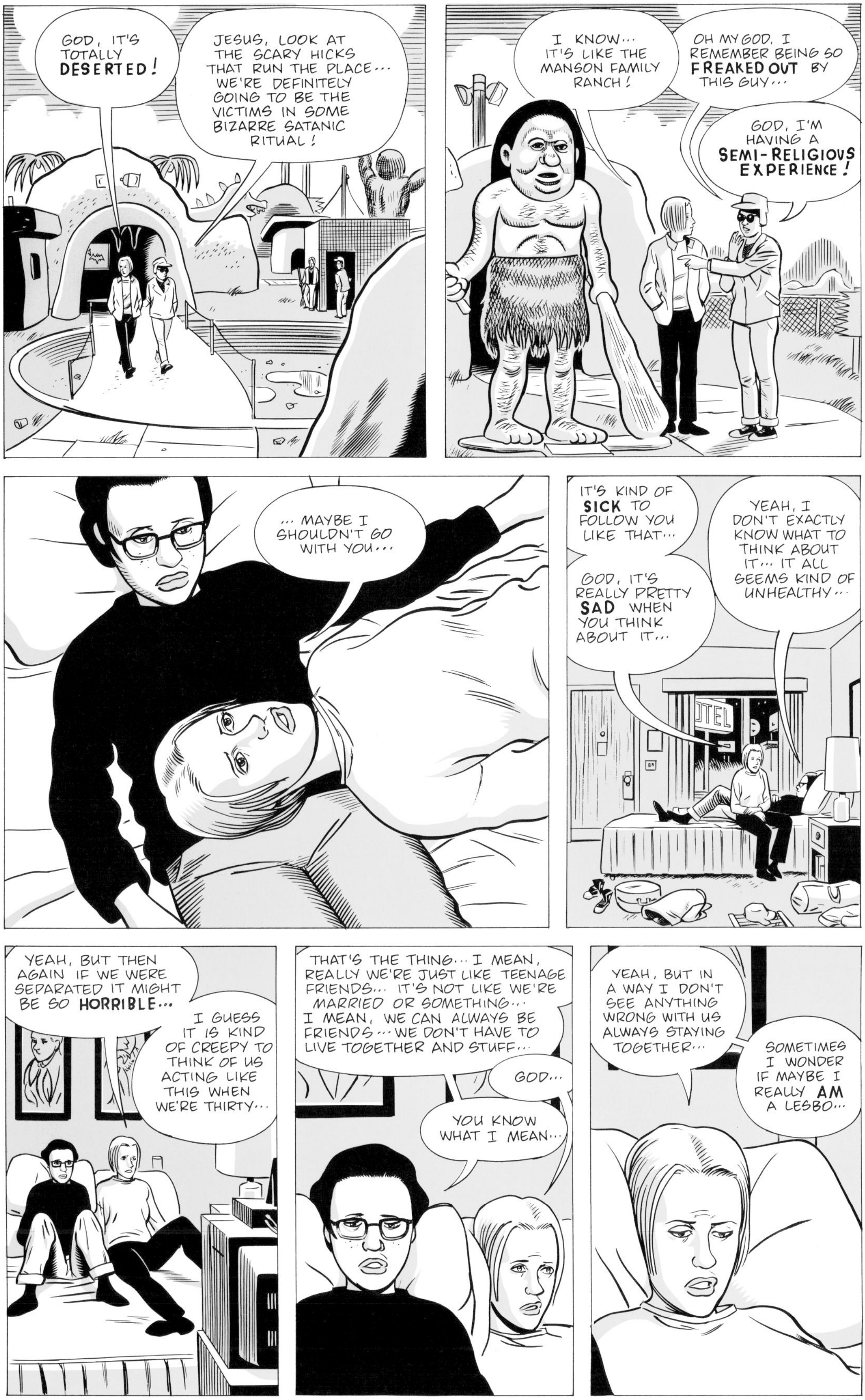
GOD, IT'S TOTALLY DESERTED!
JESUS, LOOK AT THE SCARY HICKS THAT RUN THE PLACE... WE'RE DEFINITELY GOING TO BE THE VICTIMS IN SOME BIZARRE SATANIC RITUAL!
I KNOW... IT'S LIKE THE MANSON FAMILY RANCH!
OH MY GOD, I REMEMBER BEING SO FREAKED OUT BY THIS GUY...
GOD, I'M HAVING A SEMI-RELIGIOUS EXPERIENCE!
... MAYBE I SHOULDN'T GO WITH YOU...
IT'S KIND OF SICK TO FOLLOW YOU LIKE THAT...
GOD, IT'S REALLY PRETTY SAD WHEN YOU THINK ABOUT IT...
YEAH, I DON'T EXACTLY KNOW WHAT TO THINK ABOUT IT... IT ALL SEEMS KIND OF UNHEALTHY...
YEAH, BUT THEN AGAIN IF WE WERE SEPARATED IT MIGHT BE SO HORRIBLE...
I GUESS IT IS KIND OF CREEPY TO THINK OF US ACTING LIKE THIS WHEN WE'RE THIRTY...
THAT'S THE THING... I MEAN, REALLY WE'RE JUST LIKE TEENAGE FRIENDS... IT'S NOT LIKE WE'RE MARRIED OR SOMETHING... I MEAN, WE CAN ALWAYS BE FRIENDS... WE DON'T HAVE TO LIVE TOGETHER AND STUFF...
GOD...
YOU KNOW WHAT I MEAN...
YEAH, BUT IN A WAY I DON'T SEE ANYTHING WRONG WITH US ALWAYS STAYING TOGETHER...
SOMETIMES I WONDER IF MAYBE I REALLY AM A LESBO...

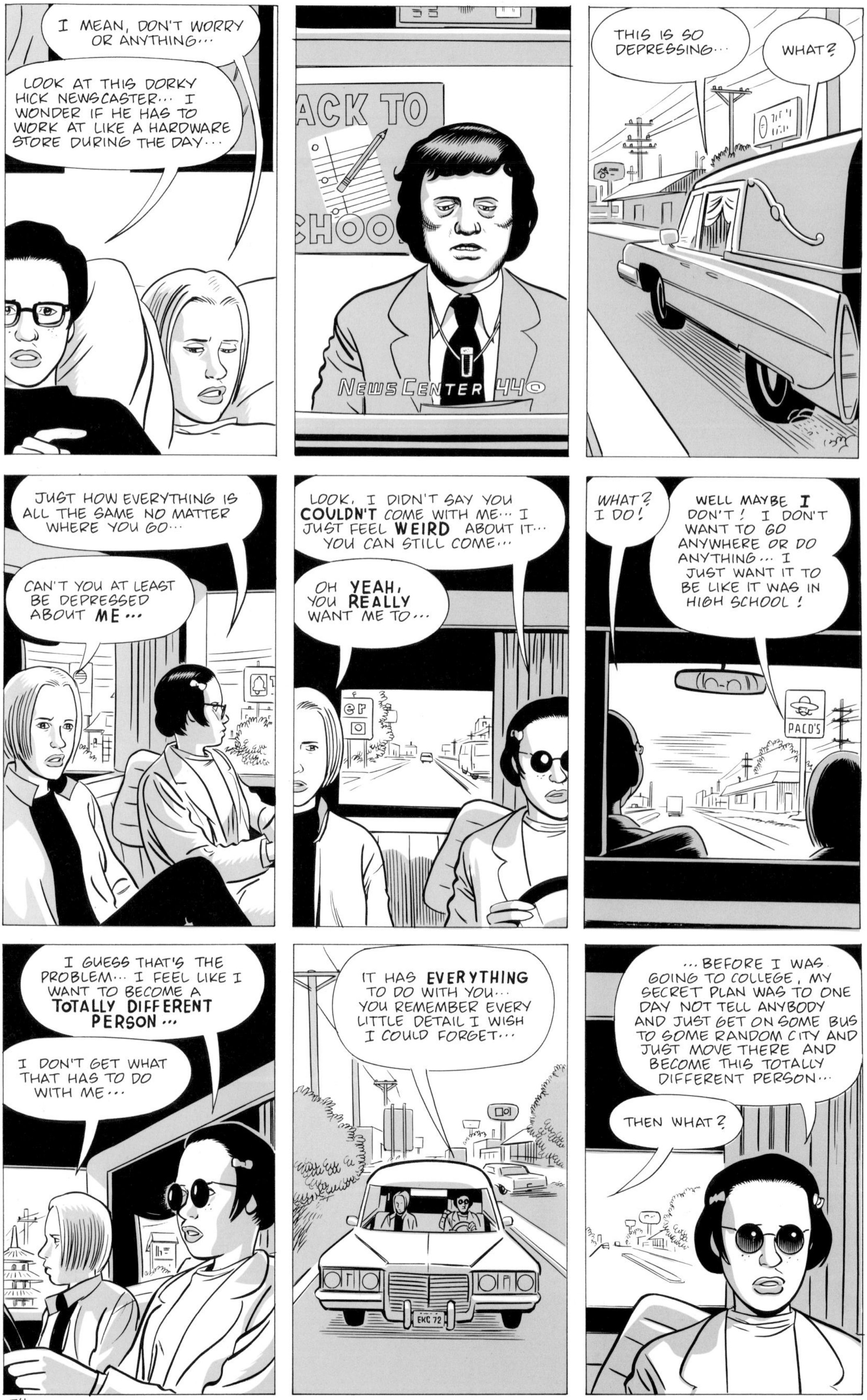
I MEAN, DON'T WORRY OR ANYTHING...
LOOK AT THIS DORKY HICK NEWSCASTER... I WONDER IF HE HAS TO WORK AT LIKE A HARDWARE STORE DURING THE DAY...
NEWS CENTER 44
THIS IS SO DEPRESSING...
WHAT?
JUST HOW EVERYTHING IS ALL THE SAME NO MATTER WHERE YOU GO...
CAN'T YOU AT LEAST BE DEPRESSED ABOUT ME...
LOOK, I DIDN'T SAY YOU COULDN'T COME WITH ME... I JUST FEEL WEIRD ABOUT IT... YOU CAN STILL COME...
OH YEAH, YOU REALLY WANT ME TO...
WHAT? I DO!
WELL MAYBE I DON'T! I DON'T WANT TO GO ANYWHERE OR DO ANYTHING... I JUST WANT IT TO BE LIKE IT WAS IN HIGH SCHOOL!
PACO'S
I GUESS THAT'S THE PROBLEM... I FEEL LIKE I WANT TO BECOME A TOTALLY DIFFERENT PERSON...
I DON'T GET WHAT THAT HAS TO DO WITH ME...
IT HAS EVERYTHING TO DO WITH YOU... YOU REMEMBER EVERY LITTLE DETAIL I WISH I COULD FORGET...
EKC 72
...BEFORE I WAS GOING TO COLLEGE, MY SECRET PLAN WAS TO ONE DAY NOT TELL ANYBODY AND JUST GET ON SOME BUS TO SOME RANDOM CITY AND JUST MOVE THERE AND BECOME THIS TOTALLY DIFFERENT PERSON...
THEN WHAT?

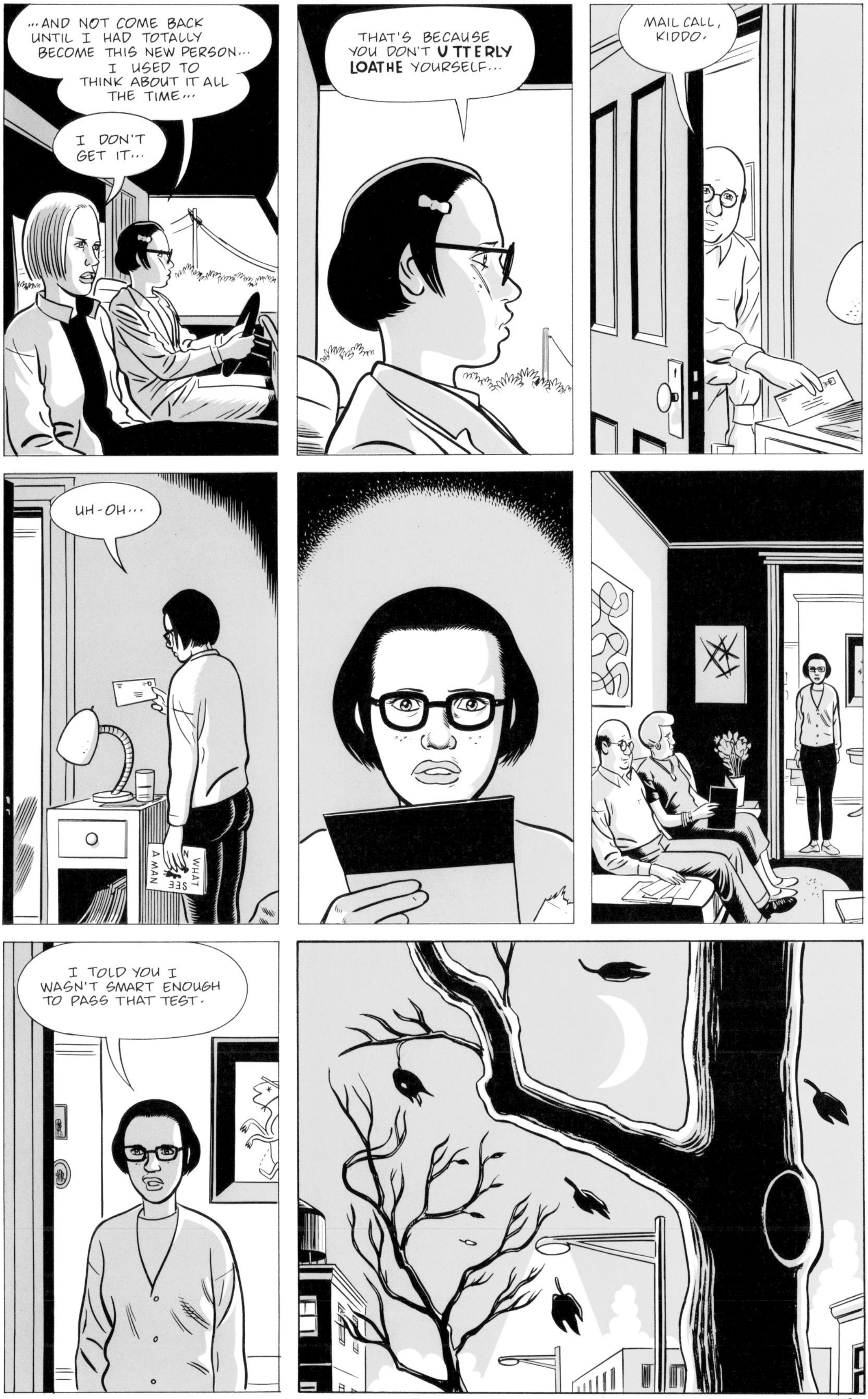
...AND NOT COME BACK UNTIL I HAD TOTALLY BECOME THIS NEW PERSON... I USED TO THINK ABOUT IT ALL THE TIME...
I DON'T GET IT...
THAT'S BECAUSE YOU DON'T UTTERLY LOATHE YOURSELF...
MAIL CALL, KIDDO.
UH-OH...
WHAT MAN SEE A MAN
I TOLD YOU I WASN'T SMART ENOUGH TO PASS THAT TEST.

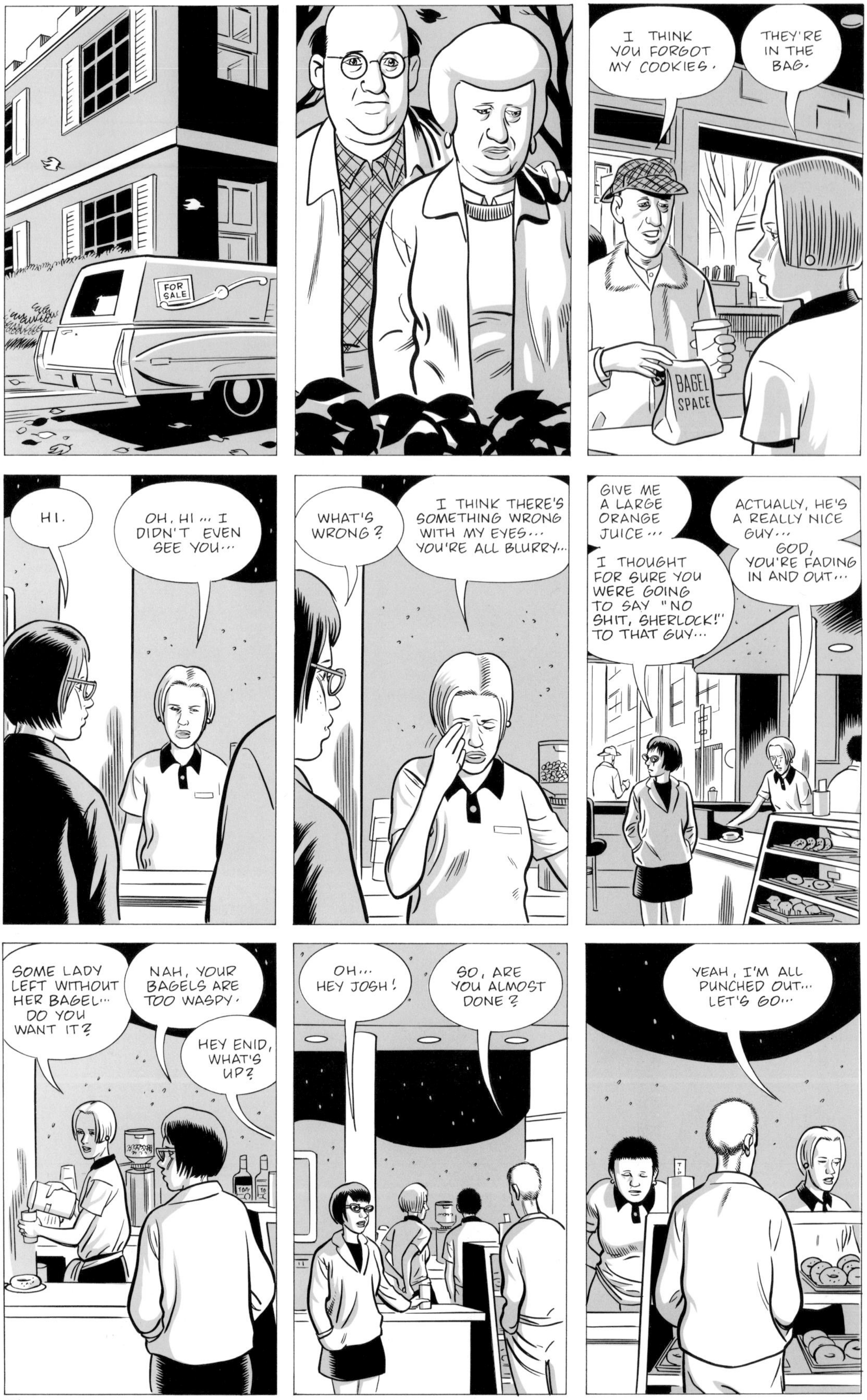

FOR SALE
I THINK YOU FORGOT MY COOKIES.
THEY'RE IN THE BAG.
BAGEL SPACE
HI.
OH, HI... I DIDN'T EVEN SEE YOU...
WHAT'S WRONG?
I THINK THERE'S SOMETHING WRONG WITH MY EYES... YOU'RE ALL BLURRY...
GIVE ME A LARGE ORANGE JUICE...
I THOUGHT FOR SURE YOU WERE GOING TO SAY "NO SHIT, SHERLOCK!" TO THAT GUY...
ACTUALLY, HE'S A REALLY NICE GUY...
GOD, YOU'RE FADING IN AND OUT...
SOME LADY LEFT WITHOUT HER BAGEL... DO YOU WANT IT?
NAH, YOUR BAGELS ARE TOO WASPY.
HEY ENID, WHAT'S UP?
OH... HEY JOSH!
SO, ARE YOU ALMOST DONE?
YEAH, I'M ALL PUNCHED OUT... LET'S GO...

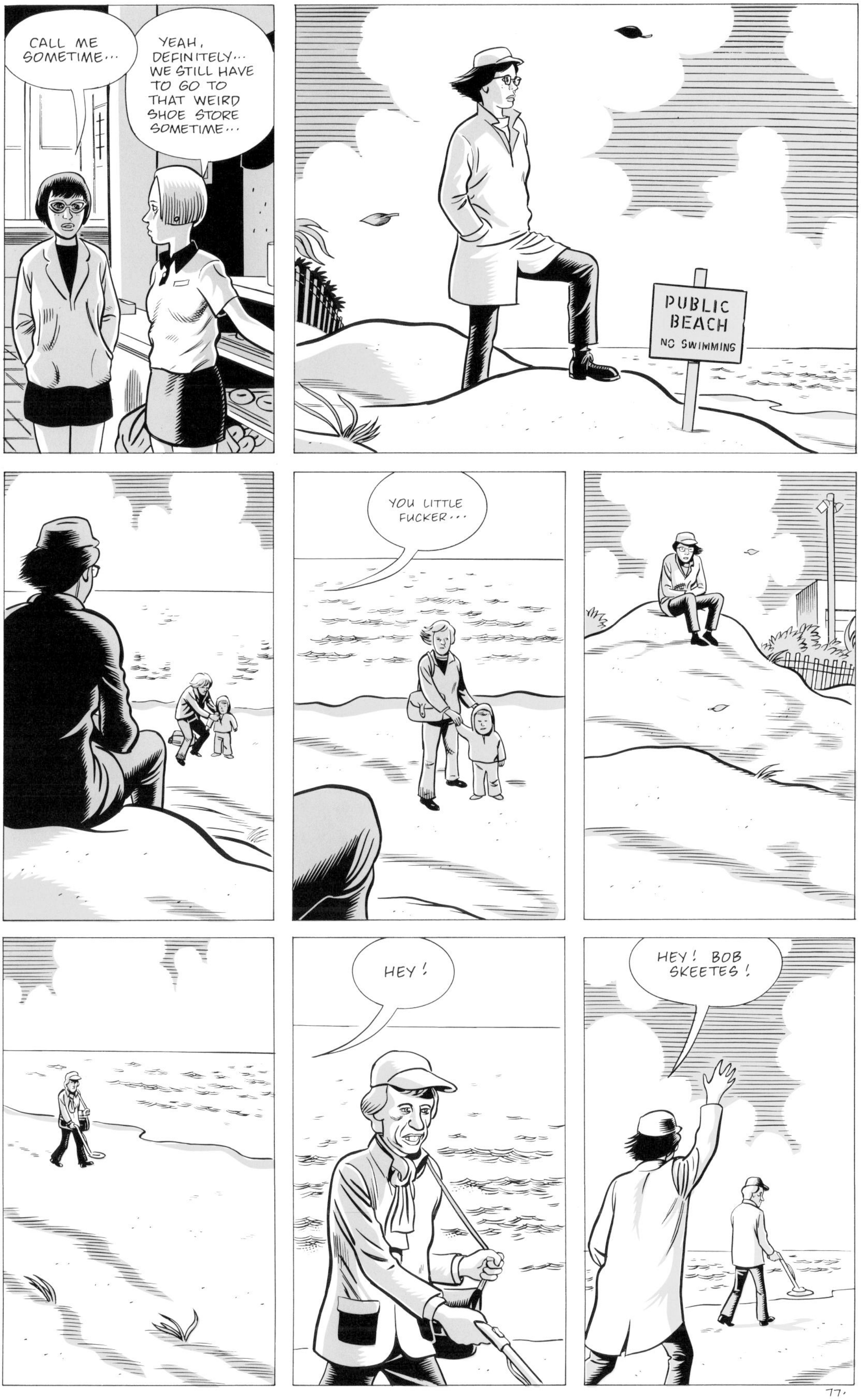
CALL ME SOMETIME...
YEAH, DEFINITELY... WE STILL HAVE TO GO TO THAT WEIRD SHOE STORE SOMETIME...
PUBLIC BEACH
NO SWIMMING
YOU LITTLE FUCKER...
HEY!
HEY! BOB SKEETES!

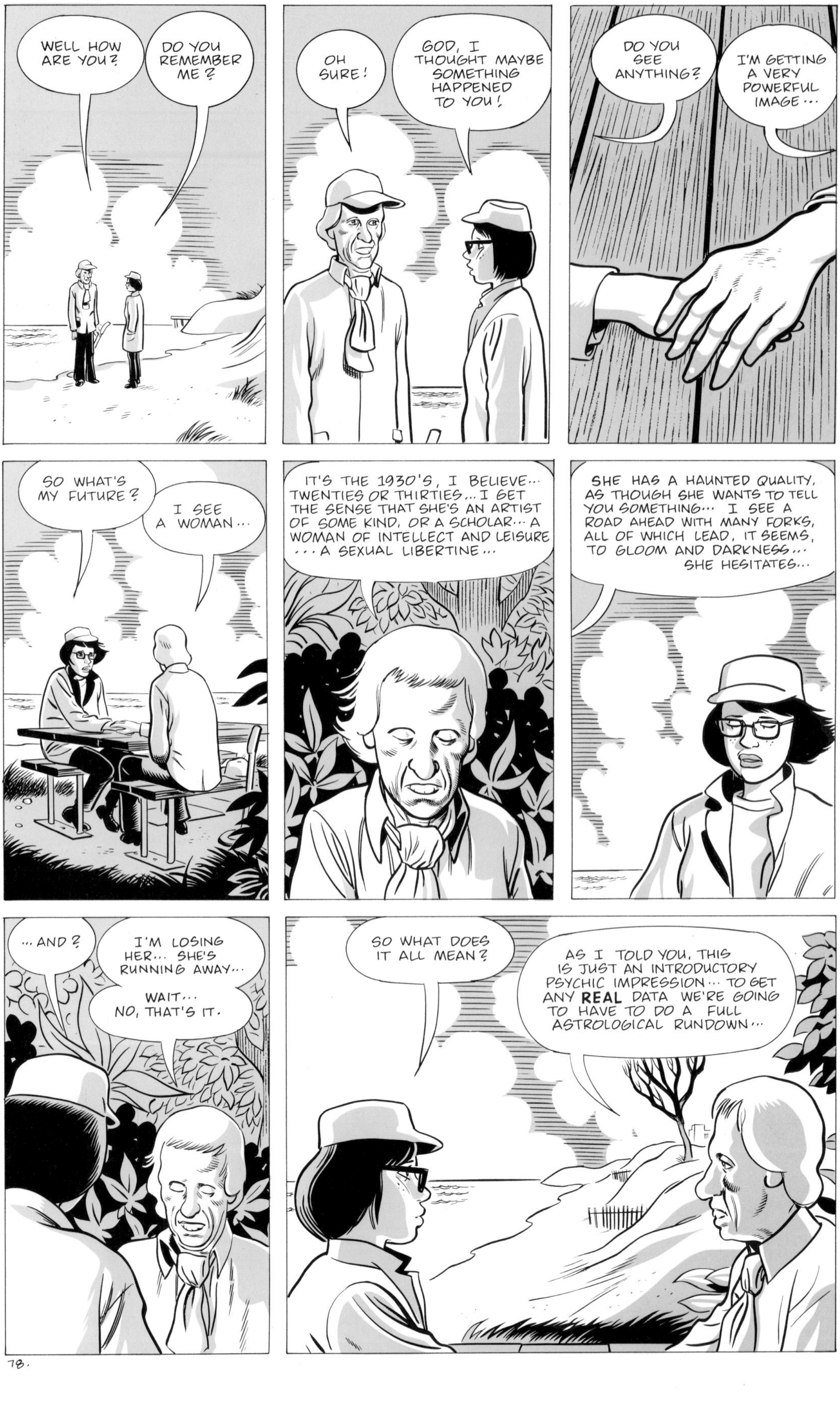
WELL HOW ARE YOU?
DO YOU REMEMBER ME?
OH SURE!
GOD, I THOUGHT MAYBE SOMETHING HAPPENED TO YOU!
DO YOU SEE ANYTHING?
I'M GETTING A VERY POWERFUL IMAGE...
SO WHAT'S MY FUTURE?
I SEE A WOMAN...
IT'S THE 1930'S, I BELIEVE... TWENTIES OR THIRTIES... I GET THE SENSE THAT SHE'S AN ARTIST OF SOME KIND, OR A SCHOLAR... A WOMAN OF INTELLECT AND LEISURE ... A SEXUAL LIBERTINE...
SHE HAS A HAUNTED QUALITY, AS THOUGH SHE WANTS TO TELL YOU SOMETHING... I SEE A ROAD AHEAD WITH MANY FORKS, ALL OF WHICH LEAD, IT SEEMS, TO GLOOM AND DARKNESS... SHE HESITATES...
...AND?
I'M LOSING HER... SHE'S RUNNING AWAY...
WAIT... NO, THAT'S IT.
SO WHAT DOES IT ALL MEAN?
AS I TOLD YOU, THIS IS JUST AN INTRODUCTORY PSYCHIC IMPRESSION... TO GET ANY REAL DATA WE'RE GOING TO HAVE TO DO A FULL ASTROLOGICAL RUNDOWN...

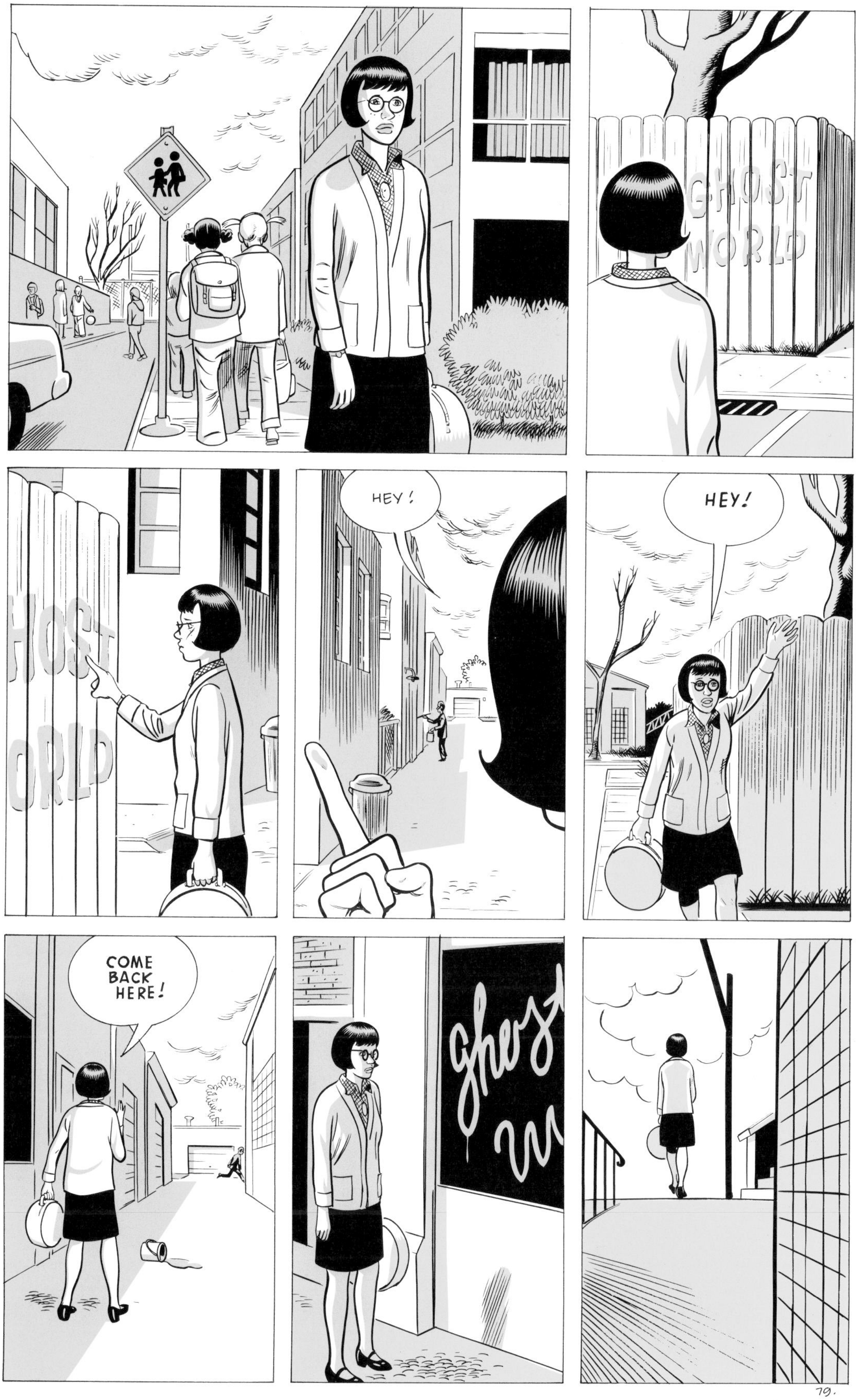
GHOST WORLD
HEY!
HEY!
COME BACK HERE!

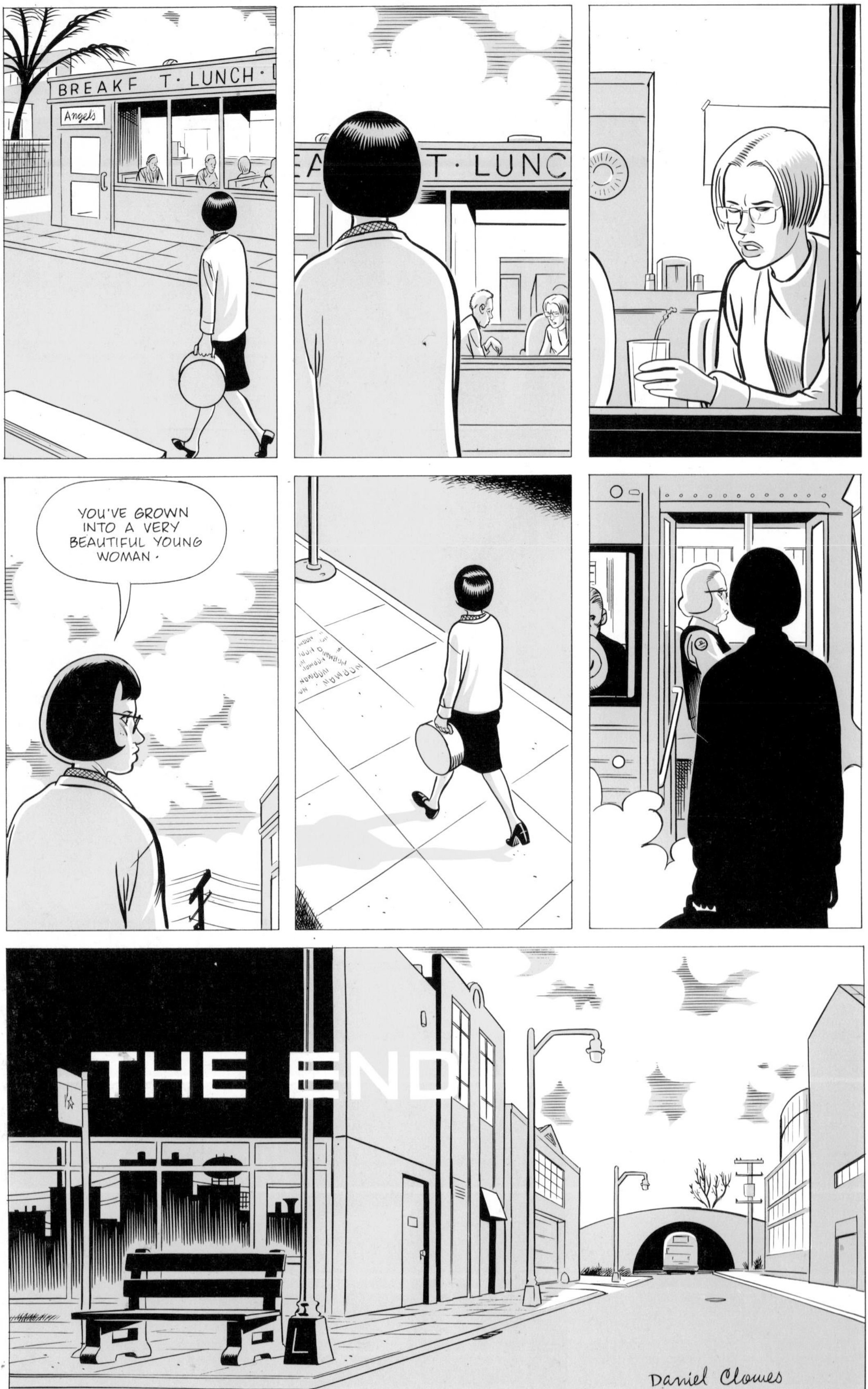
BREAKF T · LUNCH ·
Angels
T · LUNC
YOU'VE GROWN INTO A VERY BEAUTIFUL YOUNG WOMAN.
THE END
Daniel Clowes